As caring professionals, we strive to make children feel confident and good about themselves, we care for them and ensure their wellbeing is thought about and nurtured. Why is it then that many people working with young children do not afford themselves the same consideration and care, or indeed have even thought about doing this?

This much needed book not only informs the reader about mental health and wellbeing in an easily understandable and accessible way, but also offers the opportunity to reflect on these issues and rethink your own personal perspectives and understanding in order to nurture and protect your own mental health, which is a vital component of effective practice with young children. The book is underpinned by an ethos of inclusion and anti-discriminatory practice which, together with case studies of lived experiences, gives further opportunities for reflection and reframing thinking and practice in order to embed wellbeing into the heart of your Early Years practice and your life in general.

Anne Gladstone, *Author*

Working with young children is an incredible experience, a true privilege to spend time in their company, showing them their potential and the joy in the world around them. All too often, however, looking after the richness of childhood can come at the price of looking after ourselves. Kate's brilliant book is the perfect guide to do just that – personal, informative, and well-researched, each page is a reminder that for us to be at our best with children, we need to nurture the one treasure that children look to us to find: our own "play-full" selves. If you've been looking for the map to put wellbeing at the heart of your pedagogy and practice then look no further, you hold it in your hands.

Greg Bottrill, *Educational Thinker and Author*

T0268576

I feel honoured that I have been asked to review Kate Moxley's new book *A Guide to Mental Health for Early Years Educators*. For far too long we have seen mental health as a taboo subject and those who suffer with their mental health have felt embarrassed and shamed when discussing and sharing their feelings and experiences. Kate sensitively and intellectually navigates mental health and wellbeing and outlines what we can all do both personally and professionally, and how we can support our colleagues. This book is very timely and a must for every educator/teacher to read, reflect, and put into practice.

Laura Henry-Allain MBE, international award-winning Writer, Speaker, and Consultant

Thank you, Kate, for shedding light on such a complex struggle that many EY educators (often times silently) face, in such a genuine, honest, and compassionate manner. To say I feel seen and heard is an understatement. And I am confident this sentiment will resonate with others too, who hold Early Years in their hearts also.

Tanzimah Chowdry, Early Years Educator

Kate's passion, enthusiasm, insight, openness, honesty, and knowledge shines through on every page. I wish I had read this book earlier in my career. It has got me through a tricky transition into middle leadership during the pandemic and a difficult time in my own personal life, making me not only a better practitioner but also a more compassionate leader who has remembered how to love my job.

Helen Harris, Early Years Educator

As someone who has struggled with their mental health over a number of years, I can only wish I had access to a resource like this at the beginning of my journey. An insightful book with real stories from real people, proof that no one is alone in their struggles. Everyone in the Early Years sector could benefit from reading this book!

Samantha Gardner, Early Years Educator

Access your online resources

A Guide to Mental Health for Early Years Educators is accompanied by a number of printable online materials, designed to ensure this resource best supports your professional needs.

Download your online resources:
Go to www.routledge.com/9780367704261 and click Support Material.

A Guide to Mental Health for Early Years Educators

This practical and accessible guide tackles the challenges that busy childcare educators face with their mental health in what is a wonderful, rewarding, but often exhausting role.

Drawing from "day-in-the-life" experiences and case studies, this book sets out high-quality staff wellbeing practices that can revolutionise the way childcare practitioners approach their job and their own health. Chapters guide the reader through a process of reflection and development, encouraging and empowering them to create a workplace culture that positively contributes to their personal wellbeing.

This book:

- Focuses on the realities of Early Years education, combining the author's lived experience with examples of real-life practice.
- Encourages educators to think and feel positively about themselves; to identify the individual skills, strengths, and talents they bring to their work.
- Can be used individually or collaboratively by team members, with guidance on creating a positive workplace culture with a shared vision, core values, and beliefs.

Essential reading for anybody who finds that the job they love can sometimes leave them feeling worn out, stressed, and depleted; this book has been written to enrich the lives of all training and practising Early Years Educators.

Kate Moxley is a proud and passionate Early Years (EY) Consultant, Trainer, and Speaker specialising in wellbeing and mental health. Founder of the Wellness for All training company and a Mental Health First Aid England Instructor Member, she travels across the UK nurturing teams to develop mentally healthy working environments that improve outcomes for children. Kate combines her experience and love of the EY sector with a BA (Hons) in Early Childhood Studies, along with real-life, hands-on experience of working with children and families in educational and PVI settings, leading, managing, and inspiring large staff teams. Kate is the founder and organiser of Early Years Wellbeing Week #EYWellbeingWeek that runs every year in line with world mental health day on 10 October.

Little Minds Matter:

Promoting Social and Emotional Wellbeing in the Early Years

Series Advisor: Sonia Mainstone-Cotton

The *Little Minds Matter* series promotes best practice for integrating social and emotional health and wellbeing into the early years setting. It introduces practitioners to a wealth of activities and resources to support them in each key area: from providing access to ideas for unstructured, imaginative outdoor play; activities to create a sense of belonging and form positive identities; and, importantly, strategies to encourage early years professionals to create a workplace that positively contributes to their own wellbeing, as well as the quality of their provision. The *Little Minds Matter* series ensures that practitioners have the tools they need to support every child.

Outdoor Play for Healthy Little Minds
Practical Ideas to Promote Children's Wellbeing in the Early Years
Sarah Watkins

Supporting the Wellbeing of Children with SEND
Essential Ideas for Early Years Educators
Kerry Payne

Supporting Behaviour and Emotions in the Early Years
Strategies and Ideas for Early Years Educators
Tamsin Grimmer

A Guide to Mental Health for Early Years Educators
Putting Wellbeing at the Heart of Your Philosophy and Practice
Kate Moxley

A Guide to Mental Health for Early Years Educators

Putting Wellbeing at the Heart of Your Philosophy and Practice

Kate Moxley

Routledge
Taylor & Francis Group

LONDON AND NEW YORK

Cover image: Primrose, Sienna and Romeo are triplets aged seven years old, their sister Valentina is four. They love to write and draw and are always drawing pictures for their family and friends. To create their artwork they used an array of markers and felt tips. We looked at Laura Henry Allain's book, My Skin, Your Skin and then talked about the people who had shared their stories inside the book, then we began to talk about their friends, those who look the same as them and those who look different. They like collecting and noticing heart-shaped objects, and they wanted to include the hearts within their illustrations.

First published 2022
by Routledge
2 Park Square, Milton Park, Abingdon, Oxon OX14 4RN

and by Routledge
605 Third Avenue, New York, NY 10158

Routledge is an imprint of the Taylor & Francis Group, an informa business

© 2022 Kate Moxley

The right of Kate Moxley to be identified as author of this work has been asserted in accordance with sections 77 and 78 of the Copyright, Designs and Patents Act 1988.

British Library Cataloguing-in-Publication Data
A catalogue record for this book is available from the British Library

Library of Congress Cataloging-in-Publication Data
A catalog record for this book has been requested

ISBN: 978–0-367–70427–8 (hbk)
ISBN: 978–0-367–70426–1 (pbk)
ISBN: 978–1-003–14624–7 (ebk)

DOI: 10.4324/9781003146247

Printed in Great Britain by Bell and Bain Ltd, Glasgow

Typeset in Optima LT Std
by Apex CoVantage, LLC

Access the Support Material: www.routledge.com/9780367704261

To Joe and Evie, you are my sunshine.

I am grateful for your unconditional love and support through the dark days, the never-ending pyjama book-writing days, my never-ending ideas, hopes for our adventures and plans for the future.

Contents

Useful resources & sources of information

This book contains lived experience case studies and personal reflections. Whilst they have all been carefully and thoughtfully curated for this book, please be aware that this book will make you think and feel, and may at times be emotive. With that in mind, please take extra care of yourself as you make your way through the chapters. It might be beneficial to tell a friend that you are reading this book and perhaps even read it with someone at the same time so that you can share reflections, talk things through, and support one another. Chances are you are reading this book to support others. Who is supporting you? Who is your support person?

Acknowledgements

This book is dedicated to those who have the most important job in the world – early years educators. Sunflowers follow the sun. But did you know when it is cloudy and grey they turn and face each other and share their energy (source unknown). This book would not have been possible if it was not for the contributions of fellow early years enthusiasts who graciously shared their thoughts, feelings, ideas, and lived experiences, all of which have shaped the heart of this book. Thank you is not enough; you enabled me to do something that at times I felt was not possible. As I started writing this book, I treated myself to a new notebook and every time I spoke to someone for the book, I wrote down their name. The first page reads,

Gratitude for: Sonia Mainstone-Cotton, Anne Gladstone, Kerry Murphy, Liz Pemberton, Laura and Gary Peirce, Sammi Gardner, Stacey Glover, Kim Esnard, Rachel Cannon, Francesca Evans, Joss Cambridge Simmonds, David Chan, Joe Benge, Julie Lewis, Jamel Carly Campbell, Rochelle Robb, Shada Lambert, Sarah Scotland, Greg Botrill, Rosie Joyce, Varinder Kaur Johal, Helen Harris, Melissa Blignaut, Elaine Hill, Tanzimah Chowdry, Fifi Benham, Laura Henry-Allain, Sally Wright, Louise Roberts, Sarah Sutton, Sharon Makin, Rachel Macbeth Webb, Rob Fox, Jenny Ainsworth, Karen Norton, Lesley Tait, Kelly Sheils, Vanessa Dooley, and Lisa Gallier.

Thank you to the best, most talented illustrators in the land – Primrose Lewis, Sienna Lewis, Romeo Lewis, and Valentina Lewis.

Thank you, Sonia Mainstone-Cotton for writing your book on emotional wellbeing, finding your book made such a difference to me it is a privilege to carry on the conversation and encourage others to do the same. Thank you to Clare Ashworth and everyone at Routledge who has made this possible.

Thank you to Anne Gladstone for showing me how to believe in myself. To Kerry and Liz for the friendship, laughter, tears, and support.

Foreword

For this series, we wanted to have one of the first books in the collection exploring the wellbeing of staff. We can only look after and enhance the wellbeing of children if we are paying attention to and looking after our own wellbeing. There are still very few books on the market explicitly looking at early years staff wellbeing; I wrote one of the others! It is timely to have Kate's book taking the conversation further and increasing the discussion around how and why we need to focus on our mental wellbeing.

Throughout this book, Kate helps us to understand and think about what impacts our mental wellbeing. She shares with us her insight and knowledge around recognising, paying attention to, and looking after our mental health, just as we need to do with our physical health. Kate challenges the taboo of talking about mental health and mental illness and encourages us to be both open and honest in our discussions.

Kate shares her own experiences within the book and she also draws on the voices of many others, offering insights, ideas, and experiences from a wide variety of practitioners across the country and in all aspects of early years. These many voices help us see and hear many varied ways of offering support, suggesting strategies that have helped and input that has really made a difference.

This book is beneficial for managers and leadership; often managers ask: *how can I help my staff's wellbeing?* Kate provides valuable ideas around policy and practical ways to support staff teams, navigating a variety of topics and offering suggestions and tips. At the heart of this book is an encouragement to see mental health as a subject we should all openly pay attention to, discuss, and support one another with, and an area where we all need to recognise the possibility of becoming mentally ill and the warning signs around that.

As this book series launches, the Covid-19 pandemic will still leave a legacy on us all. Many of us found our mental health was challenged during the pandemic, and many will still be experiencing fragility. This book offers us the reminder that we are not alone if we are feeling fragile and vulnerable with our mental health. Still, it also helps us navigate our way through ideas that will help us and enable us to support the children and families we work with.

I am so pleased to have this book as one of the first in the Little Minds Matter series. I took away new ideas, information, and moments to reflect on. I hope as you read the book, you can find some time and space to reflect on your own mental health.

Sonia Mainstone-Cotton
Series Advisor
May 2021

Laying the foundations of our philosophy

Introduction

Outline of the book

This book is a guide for embedding wellbeing at the heart of your EY practice and can be used either individually or collaboratively as part of a team. It is organised into two parts. Part 1 lays the foundations for wellbeing. Part 2 shares four core values that create intentionality around wellbeing in all aspects of your life and within your early years provision to develop your own unique and individual wellbeing philosophy.

Happy, healthy, thriving staff = happy, healthy, flourishing children

The aim of this book is simple; to improve knowledge and understanding of wellbeing to increase your overall health, happiness, and job satisfaction. Throughout the book, I have used case studies as reflection points, with the supporting information designed to raise awareness and understanding. Our everyday actions, and workplace policies and procedures, contribute to our overall job satisfaction and improve the overall quality of our EY provision and outcomes for children.

Everyone has a part to play in contributing to the harmony and culture of the provision they choose to work in. This book will provide you with information that sets out high-quality indicators of practice, allowing you to reflect and review your individual role and influence within your team and consider your everyday practice, systems, and operational procedures.

DOI: 10.4324/9781003146247-2

This book sets out principles and intentions we can live by to motivate ourselves and our colleagues to think and feel positively, to identify our individual skills, strengths, talents – showing up in our workplaces and to our families, being all of who we are, shining our light unafraid to edit and hide parts of ourselves away, celebrating our own and other people's identities, in the form of our ethnicity, culture, race, religion, gender identity, sexuality, neurodiversity, mental and physical health, unique personal characteristics, and personality traits.

Work towards the same ethos and vision of high-quality practice in unison to create a mentally healthy workplace culture

When you celebrate all of who you are and empower those around you to do the same, you connect as a team and belong, rather than just fit in. As I hope to demonstrate within this book, your own personal wellbeing is fundamental to your professional practice. When we lead with a clear identity of who we are and our values and beliefs, we can find our place within a professional working environment that we are proud to belong to and be a part of, where wellbeing is at the heart of our practice.

Over the years, there have been very many different names to call anyone who works with children – when I left school, I was a nursery nurse; a few years later, I was an early years practitioner. I might have also been known as a childminder, babysitter; you know, the ones that get to sit and play with the kids all day. Other days I am a teacher, a play friend, or early years professional. As the early years and childcare sector has grown, so has the quest to professionalise the qualifications and job titles. Often, we feel a sense of frustration about how early years childcare settings are perceived because we know our role is so much more than childcare. The term I have chosen in this book is early years educators. I believe that we all have a part to play in empowering ourselves and each other, and elevating the profession that has become our life's work. Whatever you choose to call yourself, and whatever role or position you are currently in within the early years and childcare sector – be it a student, volunteer, childminder, nanny, owner, manager, leader, teacher, practitioner, teaching assistant, crèche worker, before and after school-club assistant – you are early years family and within these pages defined as early years educators (EYE). Please note, in the sections referring to leadership and management, this includes and relates to business owners, such as childminders, nannies, and nursery owners.

Note on statutory frameworks: while we have used the EYFS and Ofsted as our reference point, the developmental approach in this book applies to the other statutory frameworks of the UK as well, even if some of the practice differs.

Throughout each chapter of this book there are activities, reflection questions, and templates for you to use to develop and build your own wellness toolkits.

Wherever you see a ♥ throughout the book this will indicate an activity or question for your personal reflection.

Wherever you see 🏠 💬 this indicates an activity, space for reflection, or suggestion for you to use in your practice to create and cultivate your own early years wellness toolkit. You will see a prompt at the end of each chapter in Part 2.

Wherever you see this 📣 indicates a lived experience case study from an EY professional.

Early years enthusiast

I am a proud EY enthusiast. I always have been. That is how I describe my love and the intrinsic motivation that is wired within me to nurture, teach, and take care of young children and babies. My mother was a childminder, and from when I was aged eleven to twenty, our home was always full of children. I would happily help feed and play with the babies; make, play, and hide in dens with the older children. I can still now think back to that time and remember all the children and families my mom welcomed into our home and how we formed such bonds, affection, and attachments with them. I would spend most weekends and occasional evenings helping and babysitting for local families or the children and families that my mom childminded for. It never occurred to me that working with children could be a career choice because throughout school since I had a starring role in a junior school play, I wanted to be an actress!

When I found myself leaving school at sixteen with no formal qualifications, I was steered into the childcare profession route. Yes, I am one of those EY childhood professionals we are warned about, or often heard described in negative ways! Someone that goes into childcare because they have no other qualifications. Insert the eye-rolls here. But more on that later. I did have something that not everybody has; I had a unique set of special skills and talents that I did not even know I possessed at the time. I have a natural affinity with children, and they with me. I can remember once, when I was about fourteen, and had arrived at my friend's house, to find two unexpected small children. One of them was happily playing in the garden and the other one was lying flat out on the floor using their whole body to make as much noise as possible – shouting, screaming, banging, and stamping. It turns out that my friend's mother's godchildren had arrived, and she had unexpected babysitting duties, and one of them was none too happy about it and had been protesting for quite some time, and they had tried everything to coax, cajole, and settle him. For years, my friends would retell the story of the magic powers I had in communicating with children, because after a few moments of sitting close by and talking to this tiny little protester, he was outside playing happily with his brother in the garden. Peace had been restored.

The chances are that if you are reading this book, then you may have a similar story and recognise yourself as an EY enthusiast too. Children and babies are drawn to you in a way you cannot explain. In the supermarket, they look and smile, gurgle, or talk to you. You find yourself having conversations with children about random things, in unexpected places, like crouching down to discuss a giant leaf when you are walking down the road, discovering a heart-shaped rock and saving it, or unexpectedly chatting about dogs, birds, and dinosaurs in the supermarket, or stopping children from crying as they cling to their parents in the queue for McDonald's just by making eye contact and pulling a funny face. Maybe even your children are embarrassed and ask you to please stop talking to children just because they have looked at you. I know my daughter does!

Do you identify with being an EY enthusiast?

When did you realise you were gifted at being an EY enthusiast?

My explanation of this is, children know. They see that light in your eyes. They know that you see them, that you hear them, that you notice, and that you care. And when they see the light, it lights them up. You cannot be taught this. You have this skill, or you do not. It is part of your wiring and who you are. This is a gift; you may have magical powers, but like any skill, sometimes we must learn how to fine-tune them.

Part of the reason I am writing this book on staff wellbeing, I believe, is due to that gift, the gift that I would now call empathy. The reason is, at the time, and for most of my life, I did not know that being an empath was a gift. In truth, it would be many years before I even learnt what empathy was. Like me, you may have been labelled sensitive and have it described as a flaw for feeling too much and being too sensitive. This sensitivity led to me feeling too much, giving away too much of myself, deriving my self-worth from all the things I did for other people. If you have the power to see the light in others and help them, find it, and shine it. If you are not careful, then you start giving more and more of yourself away, depleting your energy and your gift.

When you are an EYE, and your everyday actions are about taking care of others, it can become a core part of who you are. You become very used to putting others' needs before your own, and you do it repeatedly in so many different ways. We are the problem-solvers, the fixers, and the light seekers. Over time, I gave away my power carelessly and made myself responsible for unnecessary things. I absorbed other people's feelings, problems, and worries. In truth, I gave away so much of myself, trying to do all the things for all the people around me and doing very little for me. I did not realise how much of this stemmed from me trying to prove I was good enough. I can look back now and see that so much of my everyday actions, both personally and professionally, were about proving myself and trying to feel good enough. Good enough to be there, wanting to belong, and I spent so much time trying to fit in; it was exhausting. To what or whom I was trying to prove myself, I am unsure – some invisible and unobtainable standard that I had set. I was also worried and living in fear of the judgements and opinions of other people and whether they thought I was a nice/good/kind person and clever/bright/funny/pretty enough. This meant that over time I was just as guilty of making judgements and assumptions about other people – comparing, contrasting, and marking myself up against those I feared were doing the same to me.

The reality is that working with children is a big part of who we are and how we feel good about ourselves, but it should not be all of who we are. It should not encroach on our lives to the point that we have developed an unhealthy work-life balance that places unnecessary pressure on ourselves and others. We often blur the line between personal and professional boundaries without even realising it. Working with children is an emotive role that requires us to give so much of ourselves to children and their families and our colleagues.

Undervaluing occupations

As I write, we are in lockdown because of the coronavirus and everyone in the United Kingdom are in their various forms of lockdown. We have been shut for months, essential travel only, children are not in school, but EY provision has remained open. Remained open with extraordinarily little support, acknowledgement, and respect, despite a general, vague awareness that our economy would come to even more of a halt if early years provisions were not open. What is incredibly worrying is that the EY workforce was already experiencing challenges due to chronic underfunding, recruitment and job retention issues, and workload pressure. It seems impossible that our EY workforce could be viewed with anything less than respect and admiration for the selflessness and devotion they have shown to take on further responsibility and risk to their health and wellbeing.

Perhaps this indicates how women are treated within our society when we consider our 280,000 strong workforce is comprised predominantly of women, who work longer hours for less money than comparable occupations (Education Policy Institute, 2020). Working in EY is still considered women's work and is undervalued because of gender stereotyping. In all sorts of ways, the world reinforces that caregiving roles are not for boys. We must challenge gender stereotypes and everyday sexism that leads to views of toxic masculinity (Close the Gap. Think Business, Think Equality, 2021). Why should it always be down to our marginalised workforce to tackle these issues? If we ever wish to make our voices heard, we need to challenge patriarchal and gender-inclusive constructs, such as how women are expected to work *and* still take the burden and mental workload within the family home. Perhaps we do not give enough of our attention to understanding the political factors that directly inform the systems and structures that form our EY policy and guidance, and understand the difference we can make.

Living and working through a pandemic

There is a real worry about the impact of the pandemic on the wellbeing of the workforce who have remained working on the front line during this time, and we will not fully realise the consequences on our mental and physical health or the human and economic cost for many months or indeed years to come. This is especially problematic because EY staff's wellbeing was already a significant concern for many. Through my work, I know how many find the role increasingly stressful and demanding. Perhaps this book will be even more relevant and needed now, more than ever. More people now understand the importance of their own and other people's health and wellbeing because of the testing and challenging times we have faced living through a global pandemic.

There is nothing more important than your health

There is not one thing, one place, one person, one anything more important than our health. Our health is our wealth. Without it, we have nothing, yet we take our health for granted in everyday ways. We push and punish, endure, and overwhelm ourselves physically, mentally, emotionally, and maybe even spiritually and live in a world and country that has convinced us that we must live to work. Some of us have learnt the hard way that we are not invincible because we eat, sleep, breathe, study our job role.

I hope that this book will empower you to think and feel positively about yourself, prioritise your health and wellbeing, and put some personal and professional boundaries in place. I have a breadth of hands-on, real-life experience working across the EY sector – from private, voluntary, and independent (PVI) settings as a trainee, room leader, deputy and manager, teaching assistant, daily nanny, self-employed childminder – so I hope to share my experiences of working in the EY. I will also share my lived experiences of mental health issues that have also contributed, shaped, and formed my practice over the last twenty-four years. I am writing this book as someone who understands the role and unrelenting pressure and responsibility of working with children and working closely alongside colleagues or families. In between the moments of joy to treasure and cherish, some of these experiences challenged and tested me. Still, when I felt like I was failing and making mistakes, they were really opportunities to reflect, learn from, and grow. I have learned so many things along the way, and I hope you will find some of them valuable and interesting as I trust and share them with you here on these pages.

MY WHY?

In 2016, my world kind of tipped upside down. I was diagnosed with depression and anxiety. I was signed off from my role as an EY and childcare manager. Some days I could not leave the house alone. Some days I could not get out of bed. Some days I slept as much as I could just so that the day would go quicker, and I could make it through one day to get to the next. I have no family history of mental illness. I suppose I thought it was something that happened to other people. It was just not on my radar. Everyone would ask, Why? Why is this happening to you? They wanted answers. On the surface, it would seem like I should have nothing to feel unhappy about. I suppose we also want answers so we can find solutions. The truth was that I think this was a lifetime of people-pleasing, not dealing with and enduring stuff, my parents' divorce, an emotionally abusive controlling relationship, undiagnosed dyslexia, ADHD, to name a few, all of which contributed to self-esteem issues and a lack of self-worth. I realise now, I also experienced some antenatal and postnatal depression when my daughter was born in 2005, which at the time I put down to baby blues and, like many of us are forced to do, marched on.

I was working in what felt like a dream role to me. I was a manager working during term time for a new EY provision within a school. The school was graded Ofsted outstanding, and there was an existing before and after school club that was also outstanding. My role was to work mornings in the wraparound childcare and then afternoons as a teaching assistant in the nursery class. When I started this role, there was myself and one other colleague. When I left, there was a team of nearly thirty of us. In hindsight, I can see that I was trying to prove myself in this role, so I had piled on the pressure, and it was exhausting putting on a mask and trying to show up as the absolute best version of myself every day. I was not content with all the hours I worked and being a wife, mother, daughter, sister, aunty, and friend. I decided to do my Foundation Degree in Early Childhood Studies, so I was working full time and studying. I ate, slept, breathed EY. My job role had become everything. I called my childcare setting, "my baby", and I was dedicated and committed to my position and determined to get that Ofsted outstanding grade too!

When I unexpectedly slipped a disc in my back and was forced off my feet for a while, it was tough to take, but it was not long before I was back at work. The first day back, I dosed up on painkillers and I sat through and led a whole-day Ofsted registration visit. I was fine. It was fine. Nothing would stop me from doing my job. Around this time, I experienced my first panic attack in B&Q with my husband and daughter, although I did not then know what it was. Not long after this, my Nanny Dot passed away from a long illness. I was still fine. When a colleague passed away at work suddenly, the small and close-knit senior leadership team and I had to pull together. I think this was one of the hardest things I experienced in my career. We had to be strong to break the news to the staff and our community of children and families, and support and guide them during their grief. The occasional feelings of stress that I had been feeling were just not going away. I was irrational, emotional, exhausted. I was anything but fine. The physical pain on top of the psychological distress had become overwhelming and all-consuming. The day I said, I cannot do this anymore, came on a Sunday, when we were at a friend's having Sunday lunch. She asked me how work was, I burst into tears, and I went to the doctors the next day.

After some time off work, I went back to my role, but the feelings of shame and guilt for being off and away from the role were difficult. One of my strengths as an EYE is my connection and relationships with children and their families. So, everyone knew I had been off work; I knew, they knew I had been off, but other than being pleased to see each other, we did not quite know what to say. What changed for me as a manager, though, when I returned was this phrase that I repeated to my staff team, "there is nothing more important than your health". I had taken my health for granted and learnt the hard way. I knew that things could wait, the role did not have to be all of who I was, and I stopped trying to force my team to make it all of who they were too. I also realised that part of my recovery was the journey of self-discovery. I developed a level of emotional intelligence as a manager that I did not have before. In my quest to lead, manage, and provide a high-quality EY provision, I had made everything about the children. There had been times when I resented the staff in all sorts of ways; for example, ringing in sick, or not being able to attend a staff meeting or training session, for not starting or finishing a display, doing the planning, setting up an environment! When I returned, I had let go of that resentment. I did not just view them as a resource – as early years educators that I needed to count in my ratios; I saw them as people, and to me, there was nothing more important than their health. I learnt not to expect me from other people for clarity, dedication etc.; and respect that we were all individuals at different stages in both our professional and personal lives.

I genuinely believe that experiencing mental health issues made me a better EYE, leader, and manager. I properly understood empathy, how to use and protect it. I knew what it felt like for someone to give unnecessary advice and fix and provide a solution. I have also learnt skills, strengths, and talents that I did not know I had. I have also learned that depression and anxiety are always going to be part of my life and who I am. I cannot get rid of depression now. It comes back and takes over for a while. Sometimes it sucks me in before I realise it has managed to trick me again, that I have isolated myself and my thoughts do not feel my own.

When I started the work I am doing now, I did not share my experiences of mental health issues. Four years ago, we just were not speaking about mental health in the way we are now. Through the work I do, I saw first-hand just how much the EY workforce was struggling too. So, I started to talk about it. I started sharing my experiences openly and honestly and relating them to my experience working in the EY. Some people told me not to say mental health; use other words like emotional wellbeing instead. The whole point is that we learn about our mental health; after all, we all have it. I cannot tell you the number of messages I receive from people who are struggling too and are scared to talk about it. Sadly, I also receive messages and questions from people who are worried about their colleagues. They can see that they are experiencing mental health issues and want to know how to support them. They are worried and concerned and genuinely care about them. However, I also have lots of conversations with people, and read comments on social media from people, who are not being supported adequately with their mental health in their workplace. They experience issues within their workplace that contribute to mental health issues, and sometimes there is a lack of compassion, empathy, and understanding.

I believe this comes from the unique work pressures we face as a sector. If we are not careful, we will eventually experience apathy and compassion fatigue, not because we do not care. Rather, we have been caring too much for too long. We are running at empty with little capacity left to deal with it, combined with the fact we have never been taught about our mental health in the way that younger generations are being taught about it now. Less than a quarter of line managers have ever received any mental health training (Chartered Management Institute (CMI), 2019). Sadly, staff's mental health issues are more likely to be addressed through poor performance than receiving the appropriate support and help they need. Whilst this book will not have all the answers, I hope that it will lead you towards a greater understanding of mental health and how we can put wellbeing at the heart of our practice and work alongside one another towards greater hope and resilience.

Attitudes towards mental health limit us and create inequality

Something that I am keenly aware of as I write this book is finding the balance between our different perspectives of wellbeing. I hope this book appeals and relates to anyone, whatever your role in EY, and to share relatable similar experiences that we all encounter working as EYE. By doing that, I hope to encourage us to open our hearts and minds and understand the perspective of other EYE working in different EY roles from our own, and who may have personal lived experience vastly different to our own.

For example, my work experience as an EYE started in 1996, over twenty-five years ago. So in this book, I combine my breadth of EY practice with my lived experience of mental health issues, which is only my own perspective, and may be vastly different to yours. As a consultant and trainer, I have discovered the same recurring issues that impact the health and wellbeing of the EY sector, so many of these issues are similar for everyone. However, combining our professional identity with our personal identity will mean we all see the world differently. It must be pointed out that we all view the world differently through our own frame of reference; we are also viewed differently and often treated differently by the world (Schiff et al., 2018). We all have our own unique window of the world, how we see others, and how they see us; it is formed and moulded by our ecosystem from conception, through early years, childhood, adolescence, into adulthood and beyond.

I hope to seek and represent the perspectives of EYE in this book, so we can listen to understand one another, and see the world from another point of view to embrace and understand wellbeing from each other's perspective. If we wish to move forward and ensure wellbeing is at the heart of our pedagogy, then we must develop our emotional agility to put ourselves in the shoes of another and feel with people. When we listen to understand, rather than reply or respond, we understand someone else's story and what has shaped their identity, formed their opinions, and ultimately their window on the world.

To dispel issues of ableism in our understanding of wellbeing

I hope that this book will also highlight that being fit, well, and healthy is not about being symptom-free; the truth is that many of us working in EY have a diagnosis of a mental or physical health condition, or are neurodivergent. Yet often, the lens of early years allows only for the light to shine on those perspectives that are considered the norm. The language we use in everyday life is important. The choice of language that we use is descriptive and is viewed as performative as it helps to shape our own and others' understanding (Bottema-Beutel et al., 2021). The words and language used in this book will introduce you to intersections of health and wellbeing that will shape and mould your understanding. I hope to do justice to other perspectives that are different from my own by amplifying the lived experiences of early years professionals currently working within the sector. So that collectively, we can all shape our version of wellbeing so that every EYE that we work alongside has a voice.

We have to bust this myth that exists in education spaces that mental health conditions mean you cannot do your job well. We must disrupt the notion that wellness means being free from a diagnosis or disability. This book is not filled with toxic positivity about wellbeing and self-care practices; I promise not to tell you that you can cope better or feel differently about something if you do yoga or mindfulness. This book is about factors that influence and protect your mental health and wellbeing, both personally and professionally. The reality is we must accept that many of us have a diagnosis and may always live with a mental illness; we must challenge the preconception that we must be symptom-free to be happy, healthy, and well. In many cases, people who live with learning differences, diagnoses, and conditions may have a more remarkable ability, self-awareness, network of support, and resilience than someone who does not. Not everyone is afforded the luxury of taking their health for granted or having the means to engage in methods of self-care and wellness that come at the expense of not just our time, energy, and commitment but a financial cost.

It is worth noting that many younger educators coming into the profession appear to be much more open about their mental health than older generations; some question if mental health issues are more prevalent, or are we talking more openly about it? If this is the case, we should view it as a positive step, but if more people are openly talking about mental health diagnoses, we must be ready to listen. Furthermore, I also hear how it is such a shame that so many young people have mental health issues; this thought process is ableist. We must vehemently dismiss the perception that living with a mental health diagnosis is something to be ashamed of.

An intersectional approach to wellbeing

There will be a combination of things that have contributed to our overall levels of wellbeing and fitness, some within our control but many outside our control. Learning what has shaped, influenced, and imprinted upon our health over our lifetime is key to understanding our own and other people's wellbeing. It is pertinent to highlight that wellbeing is subjective, and whilst self-care might be an integral and intrinsic part of someone's identity and who they are, the concept of wellbeing has been learnt or taught in different ways for some, not all. When we can integrate all aspects of ourselves, our health and life experiences, we can view the intersections of who we are and how they overlap, such as our gender identity, sexuality, disability, neurodiversity, ethnicity, cultural, spiritual, religious beliefs, and socioeconomic background.

The term intersectionality, created by Dr Kimberlé Crenshaw, sought to address racial and feminist inequalities and disadvantage through critical race theory and shows us how the overlap and intersection of these multiple identities combine to create privilege and disadvantage. "Intersectionality is how certain aspects of who you are will increase your access to the good things or your exposure to the bad things in life" (Crenshaw, 2020).

Anderson et al. (2020) highlight how the appropriation of the term intersectionality now often means that race is overlooked or omitted,

> While considering other identities is important to name one's experience, excluding a racial component causes us to ignore a critical piece of understanding; you cannot understand your holistic experience without acknowledging how your race shapes and influences the barriers you will face when your other identities intersect.

For example, there are parts of my identity that afford me great privilege. I am a middle-class, cisgender woman, racialised as white. There are also parts of my identity that might put me at a disadvantage and, in some ways, my views are marginalised, as I am dyslexic and have a diagnosed mental health condition. As a child, I grew up with a working-class background, and my parents divorced when I was a child. Talking about privilege can make us feel uncomfortable. I know it used to make me feel uncomfortable. I have learnt, it is not about thinking we are better than someone else, or that there have not been struggles or that you have not worked hard to have the things you have in life or do not deserve them. Rather it enables us to notice that the things we may have achieved were not made more challenging because of that privilege; there were fewer obstacles in our way. This also enables us to understand that the society we live in is not an equal playing field, so the intersections of a person's identity may create barriers, and it is not just merely about working hard and/or trying harder.

This is helpful and important because even though we may wish to treat everyone the same and like to think everyone has an equal opportunity in the world, that is not always the case. If we want to address wellbeing within our EY workplaces, we must seek to understand and represent marginalised communities who experience prejudice and discrimination – such as lesbian, gay, bisexual, transgender, queer, and intersex (LGBTQI) persons, black people, and South Asian, and East and Southeast Asian people, neurodivergent people, people with disabilities, learning differences, and physical and mental health conditions.

Ensuring early years educators can see themselves within our early years ecosystems

We know that the sector we work in is diverse and rich with different children, families, and colleagues from different backgrounds, cultures, ethnicities, and religions. We have the opportunity to work alongside other people with different experiences of life than our own. If we are lucky, we share, learn, and grow from each other in all sorts of ways. This is also an opportunity to reflect how differently others see the world from our own unique perspective, which has formed over our lifetime and been shaped by many different factors, such as where we were born, where we were raised, the values and beliefs of our family, cultural, spiritual, and religious views, education, our socioeconomic background, illness, disability, neurodiversity, gender identity, sexuality.

Due to the stigma that exists around mental health, we do not talk freely enough or open up about it. We are walking around pretending that we do not know that one in four people experience mental health issues, and in the workplace one in six of our colleagues are experiencing mental health issues; we can longer pretend or tiptoe around this subject. This book is not just about prevention and intervention. We have to take a good long look around our EY environments to understand why people are becoming unwell and strive for prevention, early intervention, and signposting, rather than reactionary and crisis management when someone is ill. This book is also about acceptance and hope because the truth is, we all know, like, love, and work with someone who has a mental health condition. When we do not talk openly or say we do not understand it, we are saying that this is something to be ashamed of, something to get rid of, something that makes someone less than. This way of thinking translates into a false belief that you cannot have a mental health condition and be happy, healthy, and well. This book will show that a mental health diagnosis, like any other diagnosis, is one part of who you are. Whilst it may lead to a journey of self-discovery that you had not planned on, the appropriate support, intervention, care, and connection can also lead to a new set of skills, strengths, and talents that you did not know you had.

My letter to you

This book is dedicated and written for anyone who has early years (EY) in their heart. It takes a special kind of someone to dedicate their life's work to others and to care unconditionally. This book is for you, no matter how long you have been part of this EY family. Whether you are reading this book in the early days as part of your training and qualifications, or as an experienced leader, manager or owner who has a lot of responsibility for others, that can feel all-consuming and overwhelming. Or maybe you are an early years educator (EYE) searching for fulfilment in your role or as part of your team, or a lone-working nanny or childminder who often feels like your contribution in this EY family gets overlooked. Whatever your role and responsibility in the EY, this book has been written with you in mind.

Working in EY brings great joy and fulfilment, but the exact skills working with children demands from you, are the ones that it can take away. The you that feels like there are never ever enough hours in the day, that has experienced stress or burnout or both, a feeling of nothing you ever do is good enough. We have always been taught that children's health, wellbeing, and safety takes priority above all else and is of paramount importance. That is the truth; everything that we do is about the children in our care. But how much, if ever, have we ever been taught to think about taking care of our health, wellbeing, and safety? Chances are the answer is little to none. Suppose you are also a parent or have further caregiving responsibilities at home, outside of work. You are give, give, giving your energy away to people in all aspects of life, and sometimes you are worn down, exhausted, and depleted.

So, this whole book is about and for you. Dedicated to your health, happiness, and future as an early years professional. Following the tips, ideas, and information in this book will empower you to firmly place your wellbeing at the heart of all you do and enable you to reach your full potential. Answer this question for me, "What do you want for the children in your care? Whether those children are your own or other people's, what are your hopes for their life and future? What pops into your mind?" Maybe happiness, health, confidence, love, connection, security, and safety. To thrive and flourish, or perhaps even as far as to reach for the stars, the world is your oyster. Am I right? But the you reading these words and holding this book right now, you were and still are someone's child, family member, friend, student, once upon a time, and someone had and maybe still has, those same hopes, dreams, and wishes for you.

Yet, today as you read this, can you honestly say you are thriving and flourishing? Chances are, we so often are just about surviving and getting through one day to the next and making it through the week, holding on to get to the weekend. Of course, the answer to this question will vary depending on circumstances, and I am sure many of us are thriving and flourishing, but truth be told, so many of us are not. So many of us are just surviving. Many of us are trying to hold everything together and be all things to all people. So, this letter is for you, for the days when you have felt worn out, depleted, exhausted from giving and giving and never quite being good or outstanding enough! The you that does not take proper lunch breaks, that never has enough hours in the day to complete the to-do list, to finish all the things that are demanded and expected of you, that cannot drop off to sleep at night for thinking, or that wakes up in the night worrying about them. The you that is fed up with having to go above and beyond to make things happen and get things done. The you that is fed up with being disappointed in others, the you that cannot face another day at work on a Saturday to complete training or staying late to attend a staff meeting.

This letter is for all of us working in the EY; if any or all of this sounds like you and the life that you are leading, that feels like nothing you ever do is good enough, when the truth is you have been doing too much and for too long. This letter is for the past, the present, and future you – for whenever you may have needed it. As maybe this is not you now, at least not anymore, perhaps you have already learnt some stuff along the way. Or perhaps you have always been able to put boundaries in place and know what works for you. Perhaps this letter is also for someone you work with, someone who you can see is not themselves right now, and you are not quite sure what to say or do. You do not want to risk offending, saying the wrong thing, and getting it wrong.

So, this letter is for you, so that together we can take care of ourselves with as much peace of mind as we have when we look out for one another. Just take a moment to be reminded that there are babies your love and unconditional caregiving has forever imprinted upon because of you and your work family. Children still remember what it feels like when your eyes light up when they walked in the room, when you showed them they mattered to you. In all the millions of little ways, you made sure they felt seen, heard, held, cradled, loved, and cared for; for the funny little jokes and tricks you played and the giggles and uncontrollable laughter you shared and created. A child out in the world feels proud as punch that they can ride that bike, jump off that tall tower, make an independent choice, feel good inside, and go off into the world feeling content and happy. To be at your best for them, then you must invest in yourself too, and I hope the words on these pages empower and remind you to think about yourself with the exact amounts of love, kindness, and empathy that you give away so freely to others. This letter is a promise to you that things can be different, that you can do it all and be it all, just not all at the same time.

Kate x

References

Anderson, S.D., Stolen, K. & Venzor, P. (2020). Diversity, equity and inclusion 101. Office of Equity at the University of Colorado Denver and University of Colorado Anschutz Medical Campus. Available at: www.ucdenver.edu/offices/equity/education-training/self-guided-learning/intersectionality

Bottema-Beutel, K., Kapp, S.K., Lester, J.N., Sasson, N.J. & Hand, B.N. (March 2021). Avoiding Ableist Language: Suggestions for Autism Researchers. 18–29. Available at: http://doi.org/10.1089/aut.2020.0014

Chartered Management Institute (CMI). (2019). Managers not equipped to manage mental health. Available at: www.managers.org.uk/about-cmi/media-centre/press-office/press-releases/managers-not-equipped-to-manage-mental-health/

Close the Gap. Think Business, Think Equality. (2021). Available at: www.thinkbusinessthinkequality.org.uk/toolkit/4-womens-jobs-mens-jobs/14-what-is-womens-work/#:~:text=These%20jobs%2C%20or%20'women's%20work,hold%20senior%20or%20managerial%20roles

Crenshaw, Kimberlé, as cited in *Time Magazine*, by Katy Steinmetz, February 20, 2020. She coined the term intersectionality over 30 years ago. Here's what it means to her today. Available at: https://time.com/5786710/kimberle-crenshaw-intersectionality/

Education Policy Institute. (2020). The stability of the early years workforce in England. Available at: https://assets.publishing.service.gov.uk/government/uploads/system/uploads/attachment_data/file/906906/The_stability_of_the_early_years_workforce_in_England.pdf

Schiff, J.L., Schiff, A. & Schiff, E. (2018). Frames of reference, 290–294. January 2018. Available at: www.tandfonline.com/doi/abs/10.1177/036215377500500320

Wellbeing at the heart

Why wellbeing?

In 2019, at the always wonderful Jigsaw EY Conference, I had the pleasure of listening to Dr Mine Conkbayir, author of *Early Childhood and Neuroscience* (2017), deliver a keynote speech, as she explained the different functions of the brain. She used her hand to model the brain, to explain self-regulation and the term "flipping your lid". The whole audience of EYE joined in using their own hands, nodding enthusiastically, and absorbing every word – eager to put this into practice. I sat at the back of the room, observing this moment and the intrinsic motivation that wires EYE to support others. Perhaps most of the room were learning these skills for the first time and were all immediately thinking only of the children they care for. Maybe even a particular child that they thought of fondly as they knew how helpful it would be for them and that they could model these techniques. I sat there wondering about just how many of them would have been thinking of themselves and how they could apply it to their own brain, their own stress response, and their own self-regulation skills that would be beneficial for them.

There is an inextricable link between children's wellbeing and that of their caregivers. To be in a position where we can take care of others, we must prioritise our own health and wellbeing and take care of ourselves (Mainstone-Cotton, 2018). Furthermore, we know that to support co-regulation with children so that they can learn self-regulation, we must be able to self-regulate ourselves. This will be challenging if we have never been taught or learnt to develop these skills, especially if we are experiencing stress within our workplace,

    DOI: 10.4324/9781003146247-3

which will make it even more of a challenge. "We adults all need to understand how our emotions influence us and everyone around us … We need to develop the skills to be positive role models. Educators and parents have to demonstrate the ability to identify, discuss and regulate their own emotion before they can teach that skill to others" (Brackett, 2019).

Working in early childhood education is a never-ending cycle of personal and professional development, self-evaluation, and improvement. It is evident through the growing research and literature on neuroscience in early childhood. Our understanding of neurodiversity has developed and reformed how we respond and take care of babies and children. We should also seek to apply the same effort and desire to cultivate inclusive working environments for our neurodivergent colleagues too.

I am always reminded that educators put children's needs, thoughts, and feelings before their own. Depending on our life experience, hand on heart, how many of us can honestly say we understand the way our brain works in the same way we can explain or understand our physical health? There has always been a focus and importance on physical health. To put ourselves in the best position to support and shape children's healthy brains, we must take responsibility for understanding the architecture of our own brains. To be the role model, our children need to become resilient, well-rounded young people. They need educators, who must take deliberate steps to take care of their own wellbeing. If we do not do that, then in the not-too-distant future, the new EY recruits training and entering the workforce will have additional life skills developed by their understanding of mental health and emotional intelligence that outmatch our own.

As our understanding of mental health has shifted, due to changes and understanding in psychology, biology, neuroscience, recovery, children are now being taught about their physical and mental wellbeing in the classroom in a way that most of us were not. Let's think back to what we were taught about and the education we received as children. We may remember how we learnt about our physical health, how to take care of our physical wellbeing. We know about exercise, eating five a day, how our bodies work, safety – like crossing the road.

There is a disparity between the way we think, feel, and treat our mental health versus our physical health, because rarely, if ever, have we been taught about our mental health and to understand it as part of overall health with protective factors that can safeguard it. This means the language we use to talk about our wellbeing, especially mental health, is vague and inconsistent and still feels off-limits for many. In turn, this means wellbeing is quite tricky to define. For example, many EYE are now using the words wellbeing when they really mean mental health. If we are to understand wellbeing so that we can embrace a philosophy of wellness at work – and flourish in healthy and happy environments – then we must be able to make the distinction between our mental health and our wellbeing.

This chapter seeks to define and increase our knowledge, awareness, and understanding of all aspects of our health, which is fundamental to the quality of the EY provisions in which we work. It is my great hope that in time, mental health and wellbeing will be incorporated as part of EY training and qualifications and that there is a greater commitment, understanding, and dedication to elevating the mental health of our workforce that firmly places wellbeing at the heart of purpose, pedagogy, and practice.

We must also consider that family life has considerably changed over the last century; the way in which we live, love, work, and lead our lives has changed; the traditional nuclear family dynamic continues to evolve, marriage rates continue to decrease, and divorce rates rise and there are an increasing number of children growing up in sole-parent families (OECD, 2011). The economic dimensions of family life have changed; married and cohabiting couples both work. This can be represented within the growth of the early years and childcare sector, where the demand for childcare provision over the last twenty years has grown. More families now need two wages to live on, so both parents have to work; therefore, sole-parent families living on a single wage are a cause for concern. Data show that the majority of the EY workforce is in a position of high financial insecurity, as pay is so low, and many also claim benefits and tax credits (Bonetti, 2019). It has to be highlighted and strongly questioned that the EY workforce plays the most crucial and essential role in the developmental stages of a child's life, whilst many are often living in poverty themselves.

Health

Let us start with the basics. In the introduction, when talking about health, I stated that there is nothing more important than our health, but of those privileged to be living without illness and disability, how many take health and wellness for granted, without a second thought?

Health is defined as "a state of complete physical, mental and social wellbeing and not merely the absence of disease or infirmity" by the World Health Organisation (WHO).

Have you ever considered what has shaped your health over your lifetime?

The WHO (2017) pinpoint "determinants of health",

- The social and economic environment
- The physical environment
- The person's individual characteristics and behaviours

When considering factors that influence our health holistically, such as our genetics, where we were born, who we were raised by, our education, income, job status, connections, relationships with others, and access to health care; it is with interest that we notice these factors pinpoint why it is not just down to whether we are fundamentally healthy people or not. It is inappropriate to blame or credit people with good or poor health as many of the determinants of health are outside of our control.

In "What makes us healthy?" 2018, the Health Foundation introduced factors that influence health and wellbeing, namely "social determinants of health", which refers to "social, cultural, political, economic, commercial, and environmental factors that shape the conditions in which people are born, grow, live, work and age".

Reflecting on our health determinants in Table 1.1 may enable us to identify things that we may not have considered before that have contributed to our overall health and wellbeing (What makes us healthy? 2018, The Health Foundation).

Table 1.1 Determinants of health

Determinants of health	Childhood	Today
Income and social status – higher income and social status are linked to better health. The greater the gap between the richest and poorest people, the greater the differences in health.	Early childhood:	Current job role:
Education – low education levels are linked with poor health, more stress, and lower self-confidence.	Education:	Qualifications:
Physical environment – safe water and clean air, healthy workplaces, safe houses, communities, and roads all contribute to good health.	Home:	Home:
Employment and working conditions – people in employment are healthier, particularly those who have more control over their working conditions.	Work experiences:	Work:
Social support networks – greater support from families, friends, and communities is linked to better health.	Community:	Community:
Culture – customs and traditions, and the beliefs of the family and community all affect health.	Family beliefs and customs:	Family beliefs and customs:
Genetics – inheritance plays a part in determining lifespan, healthiness, and the likelihood of developing certain illnesses.	Family history:	Family history:
Personal behaviour and coping skills – balanced eating, keeping active, smoking, drinking, and how we deal with life's stresses and challenges all affect health.	Lifestyle:	Lifestyle:
Health services – access and use of services that prevent and treat disease influences health.	Health care:	Health care:
Gender – men and women suffer from different types of diseases at different ages.	Gender identity:	Gender identity:

Blackfoot beliefs instead of Maslow

You are probably familiar with Maslow's Hierarchy of Needs (1943), a western psychological theory developed by Abraham Maslow; stating as humans, we all have different levels of needs that are tiered within a triangle, as a hierarchy of need. We start with the basics: Physiological needs, biological and physical essentials – that are food, water, sleep, and clothing. Then we need Safety – health, home, resources, career. Love and Belonging is connection, friends and family, place within our community, school, and work. Esteem – respect from others, respect for ourselves, personal-identity, self-worth. Self-actualisation – is the pinnacle whereby we reach our full potential.

In the work that I do, Maslow is a consistent reference. I am sure that many of you reading this book will also be familiar with Maslow in relation to early childhood developmental theory. However, there is more to this theory than you may realise, especially when you understand where

Figure 1.1 Maslow's hierarchy of needs

it originated and the contradictions that Maslow's theory perpetuates. It is relevant to point out that Maslow developed the hierarchy of needs for western culture, focusing on our *individual needs first*. However, other perspectives reject the notion that our basic needs start with ourselves and that our connection for and to others – our community, in which we are wired from birth – should form part of our basic needs (Lieberman, 2013).

Breath of life theory, Blackfoot Nation, translated from Siksika Nation

Interestingly, what many do not know is that Maslow "generously borrowed" from the Blackfoot people to refine his motivational theory on the hierarchy of needs. I first became aware of this, through a post on Instagram from Poonam Dhuffer, founder of YSM8. The Blackfoot people, also known as the Siksika Nation, are the First Nation in southern Alberta, Canada. Maslow travelled and visited there in 1948, when he refined the humanistic theory and developed the tiered triangle (Bray, 2019). However, the hierarchy of needs was not originally a triangle. To the Blackfoot people, it is a tipi that points to the sky, connecting spirituality and community. Whilst Maslow's theory tells us self-actualisation is the goal, in Blackfoot tradition, self-actualisation is the foundation of which "community-actualisation" is built, and the pinnacle is "cultural perpetuity", which is known within the Siksika Nation as "the breath of life" (Blackstock, 2011). The theory of the breath of life is the understanding that you "will be forgotten, but you have a part in ensuring that your people's important teachings live on". When thinking of how Maslow's theory has been developed into early childhood practice, I cannot help thinking how much more relevant and authentic the original Blackfoot belief is to early childhood theory. After all, a "breath of life" could not sum up any more beautifully the life's work of an EYE, especially when you combine the essence of spirituality and community.

My final thought has to address how dangerous individualism is to our society. **Individualism**: *the idea that freedom of thought and action for each person is the most important quality of a society, rather than shared effort and responsibility* (Cambridge English Dictionary, 2021). It contributes to social injustices in western cultures as it perpetuates that the individual is more valuable than the wellbeing of a whole community, even at the expense of others.

BREATH OF LIFE THEORY

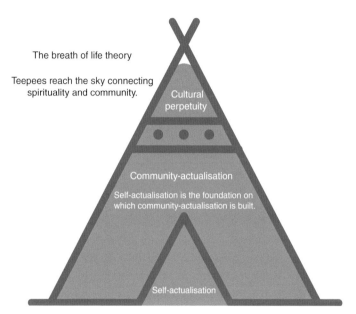

The breath of life theory

Teepees reach the sky connecting spirituality and community.

Cultural perpetuity

Community-actualisation

Self-actualisation is the foundation on which community-actualisation is built.

Self-actualisation

Figure 1.2 Breath of life theory

Let us take a moment to pause for reflection here to think about the Blackfoot belief over Maslow. This principle enables us to think about ourselves but also our community and the imprint we make on our EY ecosystem, and the imprint it makes on us. Think about how your self-actualisation contributes to community-actualisation.

Shelter, safety, food, water, and security – such as sleep, diet, nutrition, fresh air, exercise, home environment, warmth, rest.

Love, belonging and relationships – connection, community, love, family, relationships, friends, work colleagues.

Spirituality – beliefs, values, religion, purpose, meaning, faith.

What about your basic health needs? What do you know that you need to do to feel well?

What helps you to achieve this? What gets in the way? Do you need support? Who can help you?

WHAT IS WELLBEING?

Wellbeing reflection questions:
What does wellbeing mean to you?
What influences your levels of wellbeing and fitness?
Do you have a bank of activities you can dip in and out of to alleviate your mood?
What does wellbeing at work mean for you?
What influences your wellbeing at work?
Identify the intersections of your identity – how is this intrinsically linked to your wellbeing?

This leads me to define and understand collectivism for the context of this book on which the foundations of wellbeing must be based. **Collectivism:** *refers to a society, a culture, or an economy that values groups over individual interests.* For example, if we think about the EY ecosystem: in the environment we work in, we cannot thrive if we do not all thrive; if the systems and structures do not benefit us all. Our wellbeing is interconnected to our environment and the people and spaces that we occupy.

Wellbeing is not a new word, it has been around forever; yet it is a relatively new concept when considered and applied to EYE wellbeing and wellbeing within the EY workplace. Our personal perspective of wellbeing is individual to us, but within the context of EY, wellbeing has not yet been clearly defined. So far, wellbeing has only been addressed as a deficit model for educator wellbeing in England.

Many started to sit up and take notice when The Early Years Alliance, formerly Pre-School Learning Alliance, Minds Matters Survey, 2018, was published. The results revealed alarming statistics when it came to the health and wellbeing of the workforce relating to the consequences of workload pressures, pay, administration, paperwork, and financial resources of the setting. The reality of these statistics illustrated a workforce experiencing mental health issues, such as insomnia, fatigue, stress, anxiety, and a loss of motivation. This echoed research within education where the Health and Safety Executive (HSE) report indicated teaching staff and education professionals in Britain reported the highest rates of work-related stress, anxiety, and depression.

Interestingly, teaching about mental health has only recently become included as a statutory requirement within the English National Curriculum (2020). It is interesting to note that there is currently no early years qualification that teaches or raises awareness of the importance of EYE wellbeing as part of its training programme, and if we consider the way in which EY and childcare provision has expanded over the last two decades, qualifications, statutory policy, grading, inspections, regulatory bodies, frameworks, practice, pedagogy, and provision have most certainly evolved. However, so far, this has not translated into anything noteworthy when it comes to the personal and professional development of educators' own health and wellbeing. This is alarming when considering how much the role, responsibilities, and goalposts have shifted, from the ever-increasing demands, challenges, and changing job role and responsibilities that come with training for a career in childcare and then working in EY.

The most problematic issue with the lack of regard, awareness, and understanding of mental wellbeing is the human cost it is having on our EY work family. Too many educators are leaving the sector, developing mental health issues such as burnout, stress, anxiety, and depression. Sadly, the only way many will listen to this message is to consider the cost of absenteeism and presentism on the quality of our provision and the potential life-long developmental impact on children in our care. It makes sense that when staff are well-supported, healthy, and happy at work, they will be more productive. Which also translates into responsive caregivers and high-quality practice, improving outcomes for children.

Let us contextualise our personal definition of wellbeing before we move on to conceptualising wellbeing at work. Wellbeing is complex, unique, and personal to every single one of us, so what might be healthy and helpful for one person may not work for or suit the next, but the overall concept of wellbeing consists of two main parts: feeling good and functioning well.

Our wellbeing is more than a one-off gesture or element of self-care. It is an integral part of being and fundamental to our mental health. Knowing what is helpful for our wellbeing and what is unhelpful can be the difference between thriving and surviving, flourishing, or floundering. It is not just a case of knowing what we ought to do in order to feel and stay healthy and well, nor is it assuming everything is within our control. It is also about identifying risk factors that exist within our society that present a threat to wellbeing.

The World Health Organisation's concept of wellbeing incorporates:

- Physical wellbeing
- Mental and emotional wellbeing
- Social wellbeing
- Spiritual wellbeing

Imagine we were all together in a room and I asked you to tell me what things you do within your everyday life related to those five areas of wellbeing? We would all be saying many different things, sharing various activities, routines, hobbies, rituals that we live by. What one person does for themselves might not work or suit another. Also, under-standing what has shaped our health, influenced, and imprinted on us, is key to our wellness. There will be a combination of things that have contributed to our overall levels of wellbeing and fitness, some that are within our control but many outside our control. Some of these parts of our identities may show how we hold privileges and contribute to pro-tective health factors. Some parts of our identity may identify how we are marginalised, and this may contribute to risk factors for our health. Of course, we may share many similarities, but we must acknowledge our differences too.

When we think about the here and now, how we feel on a day-to-day basis, we can use a simple and easy to relate to definition of wellbeing for everyday thinking, by the Oxford English Dictionary,

Wellbeing: [noun] "the state of being happy, healthy, and comfortable"

Simple and to the point, easy to relate to, reflect on and consider. How happy, healthy, and comfortable are you?

If we wish to feel at our own best, our own version of our healthiest, happiest selves, and comfortable in our everyday life, then learning how we take care of wellness is a crucial part of this process.

Take a moment here to think about your own wellbeing and identify the things that are important to you that enable you to feel well. Some of us might quickly be able to write down a long list of things that we do, whilst others may have less of an idea. Think about how you can develop your own personal wellness toolkit of things that you use as a bank of activities, if you like, of things that protect and promote your wellness. Some ideas are given on page 89.

WHAT CONTRIBUTES TO YOUR WELLNESS?

Physical Wellbeing

Social Wellbeing

Mental & Emotional Wellbeing

Spiritual Wellbeing

Selfcare is not a one-size-fits-all model

 VARINDER'S STORY

Being a practising Sikh and someone actively learning more about my faith and trying to implement this in life has offered me prayer, meditation (Simran), the mindset of faith over fear, which has supported me mentally and emotionally with the turbulence of teaching. Some of the physical elements are also eating a vegetarian diet and mostly home-cooked foods, which support my health and immune system, sourcing local and organic produce. Keeping active supports me physically and mentally – being able to go out into nature, going for a walk and having some time to myself. Also, my faith encourages me to carry out my professional role holistically, to support children mentally, emotionally, physically, spiritually as well as academically, as we are educating future generations who will engage in society – the skills of Maths and English will only take them so far, but the values of a polite, respectful, and caring being will take them further. My values motivate me to build relationships with parents/carers and communicate honestly and openly with colleagues; how we can support children, what steps to take with any difficulties we face.

Varinder Kaur Johal is a teacher and writer. Instagram @learnwithmisskaur

 MELISSA'S STORY

Teacher training is hard. They say you need to rest and take time for yourself on the weekends, but simultaneously, you have a very long checklist of writing tasks that need to be completed for the next week. It is hard to find that work-life balance, and for me, I suffered a few falls and emotional knocks before I found out what works for me. Personally, to protect me from burnout as a neurodivergent EYE, I set up some boundaries. I set up boundaries because I know the value that I hold, and I know that this will support those around me.

1. Don't respond to work texts or emails after working hours. If it is an emergency, they will call.
2. Plan in your weekly diary the things that YOU want to do for YOURSELF. For me, this was planning on going to the gym before school. It wasn't about the exercise. It was more for the mental and emotional boost that exercising gave me. I made sure to do this and not feel guilty about it. I would play my favourite playlist and forget about the worries for an hour or so.
3. Talk to friends who can support you. Wow, my network carried me. I had difficult days/weeks, and having someone just to listen and validate my feelings helped me.
4. Get outside – when you spend your weekend planning all those lessons and you realise it's almost escaped, get out. Go for a walk with a friend. This brought me so much joy. Nature and fresh air, it is healing.

Melissa Blignaut is a SEND advocate and SEND Primary teacher in training. Instagram @iteachsen

What is wellbeing in the workplace?

The International Labour Organization (2021) conceptualises wellbeing at work as:

> all the related aspects of working life, from the quality and safety of the physical environment, to how workers feel about their work, their working environment, the climate at work and work organization.

Our job should have a positive impact on our health. Going to work can enable us to feel good about ourselves, creating a purpose and a career that enables us to develop and showcase our abilities, skills, strengths, and talents. Having a job enables us to earn money, support ourselves financially, and contribute to the world around us. We should all have the opportunity to work in a job role that allows us to show all of who we are and what we have to offer and share with the world. So often, we hide huge parts of our identity, edit ourselves, hide our light, and stay small so we can stay safe. When we do this, people miss the opportunity of really knowing us, but it also leads to us not really seeing all of who someone else is and what they have to offer either. Unfortunately, we know stigma and discrimination exist within workplaces, whether covertly or more overtly, so we may behave like this because of past experiences that have not been positive.

Let us consider wellbeing in the workplace from an EY perspective so that we can conceptualise our very own early years definition. In the simplest terms, wellbeing in the workplace can be thought of as how happy, healthy, and comfortable we feel at work. The truth is, it is much more complex than that. When we face issues within work that affect our wellbeing it can be difficult.

I believe the factors that cause wellbeing issues in our EY environments all lead to the same recurring themes and issues. I address them by using four core values to consider risk and protective factors for wellbeing, which are from Part 2 of this book. When we understand our EY risk factors, it requires professional development and personal development based on principles of collectivism.

Those areas are:

- A vision of team togetherness
- Connection and belonging
- Health and harmony
- A culture of kindness and accountability

It is important to note here that when thinking about lone workers, childminders, and nannies, wellbeing issues are still present. These can develop from some of the same common and recurring themes that exist within private, voluntary, and independent (PVI) settings. Interestingly, they relate back to everyday practice and pedagogy. So yes, how well staff are supported and provided with all the necessary information, training, and support to fulfil their role is crucial; but if you work alone or are the owner, manager or leader and are thinking, "What about me?" "Who looks after me?", then the answer is *you* do! If we look at the big stuff, reflect and focus on what is causing us worry, uncertainty, or inconsistency, then we cultivate protective factors to address the situation and improve wellbeing.

What is the big stuff, then? It is your pedagogy: the everyday ethos and philosophy that you follow, that underpins all you do. In the words of Vanessa Dooley, "every day is a learning day"; it is all about the quality of your provision and the impact it has on your whole community. It is a consistent, ongoing everyday practice that embeds high-quality practice, policies, and procedures that leads to job satisfaction and high levels of wellbeing. Crucially, this is led by a leadership team who has a clear vision of their intent and how to implement it, and its impact on all staff, children, and families. The consistent and fair management of all staff creates a mentally healthy workplace that promotes trust, respect, and dignity. The owner/manager has a crucial role as they must empower everyone to take responsibility. This includes, to a certain extent, parents and visitors. Every member of the team and community has a part to play in developing and positively contributing to and upholding the values and beliefs of the setting.

Employers have long since had a duty of care to their staff covered under the Health and Safety at Work Act (1974), and employees are protected under the Equality Act (2010). We are moving beyond the statutory and legal guidelines and measures that are enforced on us, as our understanding has developed, and workplaces that invest in their staff see the benefits.

Wellbeing issues

The long working hours and duration spent at work emphasises the importance of promoting health and wellbeing in the workplace. Investing in staff wellbeing can have positive outcomes for staff, children, and families. Studies have shown there is a relationship between the psychological wellbeing of employees and positive organisational outcomes, such as reduced levels of sickness absence as well as enhanced productivity and performance (Department for Business and Innovation Skills, 2014).

A crucial and essential part of this book is about busting myths around wellbeing in the EY. When Ofsted, England's regulatory body, published the term "wellbeing issues" within the Education Inspection Framework

(2019), there was some confusion about what this meant in everyday practice. The aim under Leadership and Management sought to ensure that factors that affected the wellbeing of staff within the workplace were quickly identified and addressed, which would reduce stress and pressure and improve EYE health and wellbeing. Meaning EYE, would "report high levels of support related to wellbeing?" This is not as easy as it sounds, as many managers already feel as though they bend over backwards to support staff, and hence it caused worry and uncertainty on how settings could support staff wellbeing.

There is a growing community of EY professionals online who connect and network to share practice, ideas, inspiration, and support one another. This type of personal and professional development was not around when I trained over 24 years ago. There are many advantages to having a community of fellow EY enthusiasts available at your fingertips 24/7. We can connect with educators all over the globe to enthuse, and inspire, and share practice and pedagogy.

There are also, of course, some downsides to the relentless scrolling, searching, and all-consuming ideas and inspiration. Whilst helpful and useful, it should also come with a warning. What works for one setting, space, child, family, educator, or organisation, is not going to work for the next. When we replicate ideas and things we have seen and oohed and ahhed at online, the risk is that we lose the focus or purpose of our intentions. Picture perfect photographs and images do not show the hard work, thought, and intention in mind for the particular cohort of children they have been planned for. What has this got to do with wellbeing? Well, we see wellbeing trying to be replicated in this same way. Contrary to popular social media belief, wellbeing cannot be simply ticked off. It is not something to be thought of as having got it done, finished, or completed. It also cannot be thought about occasionally as though it can be picked up and put down. I have lost count of the amount of social media posts I have read that say, "Any ideas for staff wellbeing?" "What do you do for staff wellbeing?"

Often my heart sinks when I read the responses. Sometimes I feel empathy and understanding, and write diplomatically. Other times I confess to feeling cross, even angry. Other times I like, love, care, and support the comments of others who have written before me. I am usually always left saddened, exasperated, and worried about the responses I have read. I would like to make the point here that this is not because I view myself as knowing better than anyone else. It is more that what I read indicates just how little people, namely EYE, value their own health, and how we have perpetuated that, as caregivers, our needs are overlooked and secondary.

Due to the nature of the busy and demanding job role, many factors can influence educator wellbeing in the workplace. I sought the views of EYE to understand current factors that have contributed to wellbeing issues within the workplace. It is fascinating to note that there is little here to do with children themselves. It is much more about how staff are supported to fulfil the role and responsibilities and the factors that get in the way; such as the lack of resources we have to solve the issues, funding, money, training, which all impacts our health, our relationships, and our daily purpose.

Figure 1.3 Wellbeing issues

The What Works Centre for Wellbeing (2021) framework uses an evidence-based model that indicates five main drivers of wellbeing in the workplace, which are:

- Health (how we feel physically and mentally)
- Relationships with others at work
- Purpose (goals, motivation, workload, ability to influence decisions)
- Environment (work culture, facilities, and tools)
- Security (financial security, safety, bullying/harassment)

This shows us how in all sorts of different ways and everyday actions, the environment in which we choose to work impacts and influences our overall wellbeing in the workplace. It is not uncommon to feel unsatisfied, underappreciated, and stressed in our job. Working in EY is anything but simple. It is complex and demands a lot of responsibility. Perhaps we also take advantage of our workforce's kind and caring nature and expect them to be enthusiasts all of the time and like every aspect of the role. My friend and colleague Kerry Payne made me laugh out loud when she told me that she has never liked working outside. She pointed out how there is strength in our autonomy and not having to pretend we like everything about our role. Kerry also points out that not everyone working with children also enjoys it that much. They do not always have a love for the job. It is just a job and how some people get off on control, perhaps especially so in teaching roles.

Neurodiversity affirming practice

DAVID'S STORY

"Just because you can cope with something, does not mean that you should"

To me, issues of workload are by far the biggest barrier to the wellbeing of educators as well as children. But before I explain further, it is worth sharing more about myself.

I am a 37-year-old middle class, straight, cisgender man who is racialised as white. I also got diagnosed with ADHD (Inattentive type) last year. As I was not a visibly hyperactive, "naughty" child, this diagnosis has truly shocked me, and I am only beginning to learn about what ADHD actually is, how to start unlearning a false and terribly negative view of myself, what this means for working in Early Years education and what sort of life I hope to live moving forward.

Dopamine is a "chemical messenger" in our brains that impacts our mood, attention, focus and movement. I and other people with ADHD really struggle, on a physiological level, to access or use dopamine as well as neurotypical people. To put this simply, I struggle to pay attention to things I am not interested in. The flipside of this is the few times of my life when I do get interested in something; I get really interested in it. It took about five years, but Early Years education is now a lifelong interest of mine, and I am constantly engaging in my own CPD in my own time.

I am learning that I simply do have less mental and cognitive bandwidth than many co-workers. But I am increasingly convinced that just because neurotypical people can cope with or tolerate things does not mean they are a worthwhile use of educators' – or the children's – time. In fact, I am increasingly convinced that the biggest and most important thing early years educators can do is less. The workload is too high. Everyone's brains and nervous systems are stretched too thin, many times with tasks we know in our hearts have little to do with children's learning and more with fulfilling our assumptions of what other adults might want us to do.

My ADHD brain has forced me to have a laser focus on what really matters for me while at work. I would not still be in this field otherwise. Of course, my privilege, financial stability and socialisation as a white, middle-class straight man gives me a firmer ground to stand on in this regard. There are much our sector needs to learn from neurodivergent colleagues who are women, from various communities of colour, working-class as well. ADHD is a genuine struggle for me, but others with or without a diagnosis get much less leeway or understanding from others.

I am grateful to find my own personal clarity and confidence in this field. We need to help educators and colleagues find theirs as well, but this will require workload being cut, so people have some time and space to simply be. Even before COVID, most educators were simply too busy to think or feel straight. Our jobs are too important to be wasting our energy and relational reserves on tasks we do not believe in. Above all, our children need adults who have the time and relational reserves to be truly present, mindful, and reflective. Cut the workload!

David Cahn, EY educator/carer. Occasional blogger and author of the picture book *Umar*. https://davidncahnbooks.bigcartel.com/about

Educator wellbeing has everything to do with the everyday actions, practice, policies, and procedures at work and truly little to do with the one-off gestures. How we feel when we are at work relates to the people we work with, how we are led and managed, trained, supported, and mentored.

Many argue that how we are regulated and the guidance we follow in EY in England has created a tick-box culture. So it is perhaps no wonder that we saw many jumping to, sticking plaster-type tick-off wellbeing quick fixes to show that they were supporting staff wellbeing. There are indeed many thoughtful gestures we can do to show that we care, value our teammates, and show our appreciation:

- Wellbeing Wednesday: lunch or breakfast provided, team exercise walks
- Staff baskets with personal items for self-care, health, and hygiene
- Wellbeing displays that promote physical and mental health
- Staff shout-out boards – thank you notes, letters, flowers, and gift vouchers

These lovely thoughtful gestures will go some way in showing people that you work with that you care and most certainly will make them smile! This is especially the case if staff do report high levels of wellbeing and job satisfaction, where staff are all working towards the same high standard of practice and shared pedagogical vision. However, it is when there are inconsistencies in values and beliefs, daily purpose, quality of practice that are not addressed by leadership and management, either through performance management or self-evaluation and development plans, that such gestures may actually not be received in the way they have been intended, because no amount of shout-out boards, wellbeing baskets or chocolates in the staff room will address the underlying issues that exist and cause disharmony, a lack of motivation, and low wellbeing.

Now that you have completed this chapter reflect on these questions again? Do you feel any differently about your answers?

Wellbeing reflection questions

What does wellbeing mean to you?
What influences your levels of wellbeing and fitness?
Do you have a bank of activities you can dip in and out of to alleviate your mood?
What does wellbeing at work mean for you?
What influences your wellbeing at work?
Identify the intersections of your identity – how is this intrinsically linked to your wellbeing?

References

Blackstock, C. (2011). The emergence of the breath of life theory. *Journal of Social Work Values and Ethics*, 8(1), White Hat Communications.

Bonetti, S. (2019). The early years workforce in England. Education Policy Institute. Available at: https://epi.org.uk/publications-and-research/the-early-years-workforce-in-england/

Brackett, M. (2019). *Permission to Feel*. Celedon Books.

Bray, B. (2019). Maslow's hierarchy of needs and Blackfoot (Siksika) Nation beliefs. Available at: https://barbarabray.net/2019/03/10/maslows-hierarchy-of-needs-and-blackfoot-nation-beliefs/

Conkbayir, M. (2017). *Early Childhood and Neuroscience: Theory, Research and Implications for Practice*. Bloomsbury.

Dooley, V. (2019). Are you ready for your inspection? Revised edition: A practical guide to support you through your Early Years Inspection and show IMPACT!

Department for Business and Innovation Skills. (2014). Available at: https://assets.publishing.service.gov.uk/government/uploads/system/uploads/attachment_data/file/366637/bis-14-1120-does-worker-wellbeing-affect-workplace-performance-final.pdf

Education Inspection Framework. (2019). Available at: https://www.gov.uk/government/publications/early-years-inspection-handbook-eif

The Early Years Alliance, formerly Pre-School Learning Alliance, Minds Matters Survey. (2018). Available at: www.eyalliance.org.uk/sites/default/files/minds_matter_report_pre-school_learning_alliance.pdf

The Health Foundation. (2018). What makes us healthy? An introduction to the social determinants of health. Available at: www.health.org.uk/publications/what-makes-us-healthy?gclid=Cj0KCQiAtJeNBhC VARIsANJUJ2Ga_1ASKDNNeEbXGrC8JW5IySNV3QJPqDoMVFW WHozAGd5cdweI8N8aAgWbEALw_wcB

The International Labour Organization. (2021). Workplace well-being. Available at: www.ilo.org/global/topics/safety-and-health-at-work/areasofwork/workplace-health-promotion-and-well-being/WCMS_118396/lang—en/index.htm

Lieberman, M.D. (2013). *Social: Why Our Brains Are Wired to Connect.* Crown Publishers/Random House.

Mainstone-Cotton, S. (2018). *Promoting Emotional Wellbeing in Early Years Staff.* Jessica Kingsley Publishers.

Maslow, A.H. (1943). A theory of human motivation. *Psychological Review.* 50(4), 370–396.

Organisation for Economic Co-operation and Development (OECD). (2011). Doing Better for Families. Available at: www.oecd.org/social/family/doingbetter

What Works Centre for Wellbeing. (2021). Available at: https://whatworkswellbeing.org/

World Health Organisation. (2017). WHO definition of health. Available at: www.publichealth.com.ng/world-health-organizationwho-definition-of-health/

2 | Mental health

Before we get stuck into this section, we will pause here for reflection and note down our current understanding of mental health as we start this chapter and then we will check back in at the end of this section to reflect on our learning experience.

- Note down the words or phrases that immediately pop into your mind when you hear the words mental health.
- Reflect here on any family views or religious and cultural beliefs on mental health while growing up.
- What do the words mental health mean to you?
- Do we all have mental health?
- Do you talk openly with friends, family, colleagues about mental health?
- What do you do to take care of your mental health?

The World Health Organisation (WHO) defines mental health as:

> a state of wellbeing in which the individual realises their own abilities, can cope with the normal stresses of life, can work productively and fruitfully, and can make a contribution to their community.

The chances are that mental health means something different to every single one of us depending on our life experience, but one thing is the same for all of us. Even though some of us might not think so, we all have mental health. For many, mental health and mental illness mean

DOI: 10.4324/9781003146247-4

the same thing and the words are used interchangeably to describe illness. Many may feel like mental health belongs to someone who is unwell, but as we learn about our mental health, we understand that our health is fluid and will change over the course of our life depending on what we are dealing with or have going on in our lives. Taking time to consider what has shaped our mental health and learning how to pay care and attention to our mental wellbeing in the same way we have been taught to take of our physical wellbeing is a fundamental part of our overall health and wellness.

Hold the above definition of mental health in mind when you think about this barometer for mental health below.

Mental health is part of our overall health – a good barometer for the quality of our mental health is shown by:

- How we feel, think, and behave
- How we cope with the ups and downs of everyday life
- How we feel about ourselves and our life
- How we see ourselves and our future
- How we deal with negative things that happen in our life
- Our self-esteem or confidence

(Mental Health First Aid (MHFA) England, 2016)

When we feel well, we are more likely to feel positively about ourselves, confident in our skills and abilities at work, optimistic about the future, more likely to deal with challenges, and feel resilient about negative things that happen and bounce back more easily. Thinking of our mental health being fluid, if we think about a time when we had a lot going on or experienced difficulties, perhaps we can acknowledge that we felt more pessimistic about the future, had less capacity to deal with what life threw at us, or how we felt about ourselves and how others viewed us.

Prevention is better than cure

It has long been agreed that there is a substantial human and economic cost to low wellbeing within our society. Actively promoting positive mental health and wellbeing within our population has been an important goal for policy, and national and local organisations. Improving the mental wellbeing of the nation will be beneficial for not only individuals but for the wider impact it has on society (New Economics Foundation, 2008).

We all have mental health, and there are many things that contribute to our overall mental wellbeing. So, we must learn that mental illness does not belong to someone other than us. Illness of any kind does not discriminate. That means not one of us is immune from experiencing mental health issues. None of us is invincible. Indeed, some of us may be more susceptible or vulnerable to mental health issues than others. As we have learned, there are many things that may determine our mental health. Thinking about factors that may represent risks to our mental health is a step towards developing preventative measures when it comes to our mental health, rather than reactionary measures when our health has declined, depleted, and we have reached burnout or crisis point.

> We all have mental health. But not all of us live with good mental health. When we experience good mental health, we can make full use of our abilities, cope with the normal stresses of life and play a full part in our families, workplaces, and communities, as well as among friends.
>
> (Mental Health Foundation, 2021)

Mental health is crucial at every stage of life, from early childhood to adolescence and adulthood. Half of all mental health issues develop by the age of 14, with 75% by age 24, and we know they will have a significant impact on adulthood. One in three adult mental health conditions relate directly to adverse childhood experiences (ACEs) (Young Minds, 2021).

As EYE, we are aware of the fundamental role we literally play in early childhood development; the first 1001 critical days, from conception to the first two years of a child's life. This phase of development is influential in shaping brains and neural pathways for life. We know that by the age of three, our brains are 80% grown, and by five years old, 90% grown. However, did you know that our brains are still developing until our late twenties? This is something to focus on and consider in relation to the mental health of younger staff, especially students who can be working from 16 years old.

Cultural perspectives of mental health

We can apply cultural perspectives in our workplaces by incorporating them in our systems and structures to encourage discussion and contrasting views of health and wellness across cultures rather than representing the dominating culture. It is also important to note that if your culture is the

47

more dominant culture, then the systems and structures such as policies, practices, and values are more likely to benefit you. This brings us back to thinking about our own privilege and how this presents itself in the spaces that we occupy, to reflect on the people we share these spaces with and how these same systems might affect them.

When we do not recognise or fully understand how a person's culture influences and forms their identity, we do not see all of whom this person is. For example, when we think back to the Blackfoot Nation theory, we see how through an indigenous or non-dominant cultural lens, the individual is not at the centre, unlike in western beliefs.

This enables us to consider how very differently attitudes, beliefs, and treatment towards mental health and wellbeing are viewed or understood in other cultures. We must take these into account when thinking of how to support or promote mental health and wellbeing within our workspaces for staff, children, and families.

For example, respecting and understanding deeper cultural beliefs to ensure our communication, tone of voice, emotions, touch, eye contact, is appropriate and helpful.

Interestingly, the theory of disease varies in different cultures and religions, and for some, mental health is known to present itself through physical sensations and spirituality. In western society, many view depression as a chemical imbalance. In East Asia, it is viewed more socially and spiritually, or as a family issue. In the Islamic culture, there is a belief that you can become possessed by "jinns" or evil (Gorvett, 2020).

Cultural competency

> To work toward cultural competence, we must look within and without for a deeper understanding of ourselves and the cultures of the people we serve. We must also act on the knowledge, turning our understanding into more effective programs and services.
>
> (J.H. Hanley, 1999)

We view mental illnesses as universal, but we are beginning to understand that this is not the case. Gorvett (2020) explored "untranslatable"

illnesses and the role of beliefs and culture in manifesting and treating mental health issues. As we have discovered, it highlights how diagnosis and understanding of mental health issues exist differently around the world, between different cultures and ethnicities. So, we must consider that a person's spirituality, religion, beliefs, and values – that may not be apparent to us on the "surface culture" – are an integral part of someone's identity and "deep culture". It is important that we do not just use our own dominant perspectives and attitudes towards mental health and wellbeing. This is something to hold in mind throughout this book, as we will no doubt turn to think of others and how to support them. We cannot make assumptions based on our lived experiences. Moreover, how do we ensure we support colleagues from cultural and religious backgrounds different to our own.

Checking in with our mental wellbeing

 ARE YOU THRIVING OR SURVIVING?

Are you thriving or surviving?

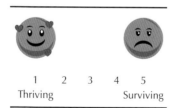

1	2	3	4	5
Thriving				Surviving

Where do you fit today? We will have individual abilities and capabilities that are unique and individual to us. Regardless of diagnosis or disability, we can be thriving and well with a diagnosis, and surviving and have low mental wellbeing without a diagnosis or disability.

Let's suppose you would place yourself near to 1. In that case, that is when we would feel at our best healthiest and happiest selves, confident about ourselves, our life and future, super resilient, and able to complete everyday tasks, routines, commitments, and obligations.

 If you are somewhere closer to 5, then the reverse would be true. You may feel less positive. It may mean that you find everyday tasks and responsibilities more tricky than usual. You may have less resilience and feel less able to do all of the things you usually might.

Think about where you are today, but also thinking back six months ago, think back to a time when you can remember feeling really healthy, happy, comfortable, and at ease. Likewise, think back to a time, if you are able, when you know you may have experienced situations, life events, and challenges that affected your levels of wellbeing and fitness.

The point to reflect on here is that our health is fluid, and it changes over our lifetime, depending on what we have going on. It is virtually impossible that you will have remained in the same place. When it comes to our physical health, we accept without question when we are not feeling well if we are physically feeling run down, have a cold, flu or virus, and we take steps to rest, recuperate, or take care of ourselves. When we think about our mental and emotional health, we do not always have the same logic, or have the same compassion or understanding, because we have not been raised to think in this way, either by our parents, caregivers, teachers, or within wider society.

By developing more self-awareness when it comes to our mental wellbeing, we can identify helpful methods of self-care and wellness that enable us to take care of our health holistically and can mean the difference between thriving and surviving, wellness and illness.

Sometimes it is only when we start to feel well again, when our levels of wellbeing and fitness thrive, that we see how we might have been operating with low levels of wellbeing and fitness. We might notice how much more energy we have or how much easier things are, which enables us to reflect retrospectively on what we were experiencing that might have been tricky, but we did not realise it at the time.

- Where did you fit on the wellbeing diagram?
- If you placed yourself highly, what have you been doing lately?
- If you placed yourself lower down, what changes can you make? Who can you speak to / has your back??
- What helpful health strategies do you have in place?
- What are unhelpful health strategies?
- Can you make a date to check back in and see where you have shifted on the scale?
- What health needs, disability or diagnosis do you need to prioritise?

KELLY'S STORY

The company I worked for had remarkably high standards and expectations in all areas.

I had high expectations of myself, and I was under the illusion that working until midnight, through the weekends and staying up at night working meant I was the best nursery manager and that it was what everyone did, what I had to do. I cared for my team, often giving myself the most challenging shifts, tasks; and, as a perfectionist, I preferred to do everything myself.

But there is only so long you can keep working and working, especially having two children at home. I started not to sleep, which made things more challenging as I was so tired. I started crying either on the way to work, or on the way home, or in the bathroom in the middle of the day. This became increasingly worse over time, and I tried to talk to my managers, but they did not have the answers; and eventually, I could not do it any more. I made a big decision to leave my job I had been so good at, worked so hard at, and dedicated half my life to.

After I left, I started to realise what had happened and how poor my wellbeing and mental health were during that time; that anxiety had been making me feel so sad and making me counterproductive. Soon after I left, I became a mental health first aider, a relax kids coach, and became in tune with my mental health and wellbeing.

I have always been a reflective practitioner, but this time I was reflecting on myself. From my story, you could blame the job, my managers or how I managed my time effectively – but the bare bones of it is that I did not understand my mental health or wellbeing or how to manage it. If I knew how to do this, I could still be doing the role more effectively.

In my current role, I am a regional manager, which I am fully aware is a position that can become all-consuming, but I know how to manage myself with respect; I set work-life balance boundaries, I make time for self-care, I learnt to say no when needed. An essential part of being a good manager or leader is to ensure that all team members know what their role is, how to do it well, and how to support each other.

Kelly Sheils is an EY consultant, trainer, author, and relax coach. https://kellysheils-earlyyears.co.uk/

Answer these questions now that you have explored mental health in more detail.
What is your understanding of mental health?
What stands out in this section?

Risk and protective factors for mental health

Shifting our thoughts from, why is this happening to, what have you been dealing with?

Throughout our lives, there will be a combination of risk and protective factors at play. Let us look at some of them in closer detail. Fundamental to this way of thinking is to understand the protective factors we have; as, the more protective factors we have in our life, the less vulnerable we may be to mental health issues, especially when those unexpected life events occur. Risk factors and protective factors are not to be used as a checklist but rather to demonstrate an understanding of factors that may influence our mental health. As we are learning, those influences are not just our biology, i.e., our genetics, but the environment we live, grow and work in, and by our life experiences, from early childhood and beyond. This means that the person we are today is not down to luck or coincidence. It will have been shaped by our ecosystem.

See Figure 2.1 for examples of risk and protective factors from the Mental Health Foundation (2021).

Risk factors and protective factors for mental health throughout life

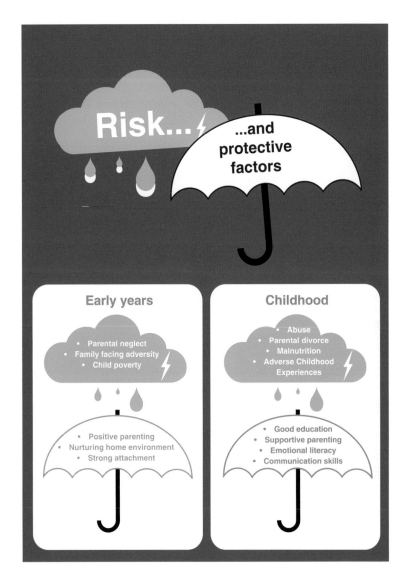

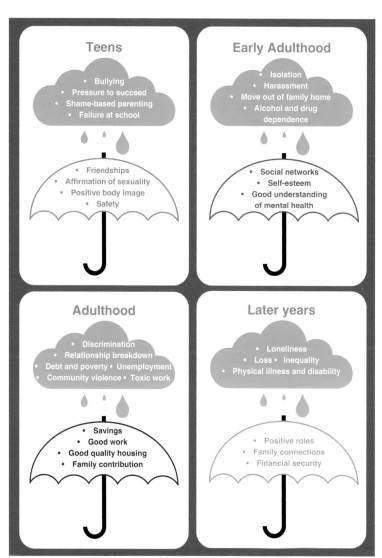

Figure 2.1 Risk and protective factors throughout life

Considering adverse childhood experiences

Research has been undertaken in America on adverse childhood circumstances via the Centers for Disease Control and Prevention (CDC) – Kaiser Permanente Adverse Childhood Experiences (ACE) Study; one of the largest investigations of childhood abuse and neglect and household challenges and later-life health and wellbeing (Felitti, 1998). There has been a growing awareness and recognition of the ACE study in the UK, and we continue to evaluate our early years practice informed by this research. We know preventive measures, such as respectful, responsive relationships, enable children to thrive in safe and secure early years ecosystems. ACEs are organised into three categories: abuse, neglect, and household challenges and then further broken down into subsections. The more ACEs that a child experiences, the more the risk increases of potential negative consequences on education, employment, and lifelong opportunities. Respondents of the study were asked if they had experienced any of the types of ACEs:

Abuse

Emotional abuse
Physical abuse
Sexual abuse

Household challenges

Mother treated violently
Substance abuse in the household
Mental illness in the household
Parental separation or divorce
Incarcerated household member

Neglect

Emotional neglect
Physical neglect

This is helpful for us to understand, not just in our work with children but also regarding our own childhood, as ACEs are more common than we may realise. Almost half of all adults in the UK have experienced at least one form of adversity in their early childhood or adolescence (Young Minds, 2019). We are thinking back to Chapter 1, and our social determinants of health and how our childhood experiences shape our health and wellbeing later in life.

Trauma-informed practice

We also see trauma-informed practice as a fundamental aspect of EY practice and understand especially how essential this is in supporting young children's social-emotional and mental health needs. These are children who have experienced trauma, abuse, neglect, mental health issues or attachment issues. Authentic trauma-informed practice is an environment in which all educators understand neuroscience and the impact stress and trauma have on both children and adults. All educators are working towards the same common goal informed by policies and procedures. We must acknowledge the likelihood that as our understanding of neuroscience continues to inform early childhood practice, EYE may themselves recognise they have experienced ACEs or trauma and may not have had any psychological or emotional support at the time. We must acknowledge that by developing our knowledge in this area, we also learn that our own lived experiences of trauma may require support and healing. This means we must ensure that our interest in trauma-informed practice extends to caregivers' wellbeing and turns our attention to how we support a workforce that is dedicated to helping others. Trauma Transformed highlights a continuum that can be used to identify strengths and weaknesses within a workplace where self-care practices are not supported, which increases risk factors for staff health and wellbeing (Nicholson et al., 2020).

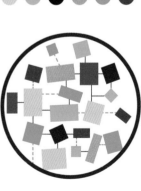

HEALING ORGANIZATION

- Integrated
- Reglective
- Collaborative
- Relationship-centered
- Growth and Prevention-Oriented
- Flexible & adaptable
- Equitable & inclusive

Understanding Trauma & Stress

Cultural Humility & Equity

Safety & Stability

Compassion & Dependability

Collaboration & Empowerment

Resilience & Recovery

SYSTEM & LEADERSHIP

STAFF & CAREGIVERS

CLIENTS

TRAUMA-INFORMED

- **Resists** re-traumatizing
- **Recognizes** socio-cultural trauma
- **Realizes** widespread impact
- **Recognizes** effects
- **Responds** by shifting practice

TRAUMA-REACTIVE

- Fragmented
- Reactive
- No felt safety
- Overwhelmed
- Fear-driven
- Rigid
- Numb

TRAUMA REDUCING

TO

TRAUMA INDUCING

Figure 2.2 Trauma Transformed. https://traumatransformed.org

Supporting colleagues experiencing traumatic experiences

IN CONVERSATION WITH JAMEL CARLY CAMPBELL

"If you are feeling some type of way, find someone that you can talk to"

K: You are an advocate for men in childcare. Do you feel pressure as a black man working in the sector?

J: Pressure from what I see. There is a lot of learning to be done in the sector. More than the pressure, I feel frustration. When I am holding discussion as a black man, being part of 0.5% of black men in this sector. Often, I feel vulnerable. At times, *I am having to speak because others that have been here for ages haven't. I am having to be an advocate; I am having to shed light in areas that light should and could have been shed before*. There has been straight neglect.

K: Our understanding of trauma-informed practice is evolving, but we have to apply this to our colleagues too and be more compassionate, like how are we supporting our colleagues, who are experiencing and dealing with trauma, as you say, and racism, throughout a pandemic?

J: A lot of people have lost family and friends during this pandemic, the sadness, the sorrow, and the grief does not hit you until maybe you might be sitting down at work, and a child's family tells you they have had a loss, them talking about their loss, makes you reflect about your own loss or losses. Then it hits you. It takes a while. I feel like the pace of things, the pace of working in any sector is so fast right now, people have to come in after all of this hardship during this pandemic and crack on. Just push through. Our brains haven't really come to terms with the trauma that we have been through. We have been through trauma in so many different ways. For instance, the death of George Floyd, Black Lives Matter happened in 2020, the protests I mean happened, and people coined the phrase BLM, but for people who been through hardship way before BLM, seeing George Floyd killed, filmed, and now having to sit down and watch the proceedings, that can hit you in a different way, even talking about it now, me talking about it now, it hits you in a different way. So many others have been killed, Breanna Taylor, Trayvon Martin. People are really going through it, even in older days, Rodney King. You know, when you have to process all of that and when you are carrying a different kind of stress on your shoulders, for black people, it is gonna be more intense. Others have had to witness this. Anyone that understands injustice anyone can see the injustice. It is going to stress them out too. Our wellbeing comes through so many different angles, illnesses, affliction, disparity, deprivation, poverty, different background. We have to be aware. We have to bring love to the forefront of our minds, we put ourselves last, and we have to put ourselves first. Bringing empathy and self-love to the forefront of our minds.

Jamel C. Campbell is an EY educator, EY consultant, and aspiring children's author. https://twitter.com/JamelCarly, www.instagram.com/jamel.carly/

Stress

How often would you say you use the word stress? How often would you say you experience stress in your everyday life? Working with children can be stressful; working with vulnerable children and children with specific requirements without adequate training, support, or funding, following a daily routine, meeting ratios, following guidelines, policies, and procedures, not to mention the word Ofsted, the very way in which early childhood provision is monitored and regulated, is stressful in itself. Let us be honest; parents can cause us stress, all of the show arounds, open days, parents' evenings, events. Working with other people can be stressful; working alone can be stressful too. That is a lot of stress and pressure – day in day out, seven days a week, 52 weeks a year.

So many of us have just accepted stress as part of everyday life, and we might feel as though there is little we can do about the stress that we experience both professionally and personally. Yet the very definition of stress is "a state of mental or emotional strain or tension resulting from adverse or demanding circumstances", and whilst stress is not an illness, if not taken seriously, it can lead to illness. Our bodies are not wired for enduring stress for long periods of time, and if we accept the mental and emotional toll that comes from these demanding circumstances, we are unknowingly setting ourselves up to fail.

Stress has everything to do with mental health

Over time, experiencing stress will take a toll on our health, both physically and mentally; we cannot keep ignoring the warning signs when they show up – we must pay attention to our body. Some people may identify that they thrive on stress and pressure, and to a certain extent, stress can be good for us. It can make us more productive, making things happen and getting things done. The difference between stress and pressure is universally accepted as the length of time we deal with something; for, pressure is usually a short-term experience – like we have one chance to prove ourselves and get something right, perform and complete a task and do well, like Ofsted for example, or a job interview, or college presentation. Stress is usually the situation we find ourselves in, like work for example, and having too many demands and not enough time, like resources or the energy to meet them, like being short-staffed and out of ratio, not receiving proper training to complete the job role that is expected of you, or maybe lacking the correct equipment or resources that we need for the responsibilities that we must meet.

The damage of unchecked stress

Our autonomic nervous system regulates three physiological states. Our level of safety determines which one is stimulated, so when we feel threatened or in danger, we turn instinctively to the first level, which is social engagement. If we do not find comfort or are in immediate danger, we prepare to go into what we know as fight or flight. If this fails, we freeze or may even collapse (Van Der Kolk, 2015). Interestingly, the vagus nerve extends from our brains all the way down into our colon, registering and sending communication between the brain and organs such as the heart, the lungs, and the gut (Breit et al., 2018). Our social engagement has a lot to do with the vagus nerve. When engaged, we respond to social cues, and it sends messages to slow down our heart rate, including regulating our breathing, enabling us to feel calm, relaxed. To be able to feel "emotionally close" to another and take care of our young, our brain needs to switch off its natural vigilance (Van Der Kolk, 2015).

When we experience stress, our body produces and releases cortisol and adrenaline, and in turn, glucose. Think of it like your brain firing up your body's threat detection system, on high alert for anything that might cause danger and harm, with glucose giving us the energy we need to escape any threat (Geiker et al., 2017). Interestingly, research links to the vagus nerve and a strong vagal tone which indicate the ability to regulate glucose levels (Malbert et al., 2017).

I also add a fourth F, which is flop! If you have experienced high levels of stress, fight, flight, or freeze, then you can be worn out, depleted and need to flop to rest, recover and recuperate. This can be related to the way in which our adrenaline levels drop, and cortisol kicks in to restore that energy. We may crave sugar for a quick fix to improve energy levels (Geiker et al., 2017).

If left unchecked, cortisol can do us a lot of harm when continuously released, which also suppresses the immune system, increasing pressure and blood sugars, contributing to obesity, interfering with sleep, causing insomnia (Nicholson et al., 2020). Interestingly, increasing evidence indicates that sleep influences eating behaviours (see Chaput, 2010). When our sleep is disrupted, and we experience fatigue and tiredness, we are already starting the day on the back foot; to make it through the day, our body is going to demand more fuel, namely more calories, to boost our energy. It is necessary for EYE who have a physically and mentally demanding job role to eat nutritious, nourishing, and sustaining foods. We know this because the diet we provide in our EY settings is fundamental to the health and wellbeing of children in our care. We are required to go to great lengths to provide high-quality, wholesome menus and daily meals. If we can do this for our children, then can we do this for ourselves and our team? For example, when wellbeing baskets became an early years trend, lots of people were providing breakfast items, which is wonderful. So, this is not a wellbeing basket; call it what it is, breakfast! You provide breakfast because it is helpful for staff rushing into work for 7 a.m.; it takes care of them and sets them up for the day, not to mention how nice it is for staff to sit and eat and chat sociably with children as they eat. Addressing stress is key to many health benefits. The correlation between stress and the impact on the reduced effectiveness of our immune system has to be another serious consideration, especially as working with children means encountering all sorts of early childhood communicable diseases. A big part of stress when working in EY is staffing ratios and dealing with the impact of staff sickness and absence. If we can address stress to combat one aspect of the impact on staff sickness and absence through prevention, then it will have numerous benefits.

Interestingly, I recently discovered a fifth. Perry (2021) says there is something we unconsciously yet intrinsically seek before our nervous system goes into fight, flight or freeze mode. We flock. Flock towards safety, security, towards others for reassurance and support; if we do not feel safe that is when we try to find our own mode of protection. In our roles we are that safety for young children, they flock to us. In the same way, we create that safety for children, so should we cultivate healthy work environments for staff too?

Addressing our stress

The ability to respond to stress and to control our stress response is crucial to survival. We learn our stress responses from our own caregivers, as babies, so that as adults, we can usually manage our stress responses and are able to self-regulate, "from the start of life, we require others to help us to cope with stress" (Szalavitz & Perry, 2010). This got me thinking about how the workplace environment, and how the people we work with and the children we care for, may influence our health and, indeed, our stress response. Research indicates that not only is stress contagious (Buchanan et al., 2011), but that "emotional contagion" synchronises our emotions with those we spend time with, and notably low pleasantness is more contagious than high pleasantness (Block & Burnett Heyes, 2020; Weale, 2021).

Therefore, if we are working with people who are experiencing high levels of stress, it may impact our own health and emotional wellbeing. Interestingly, if we think about it, we might pick up on others' stress before we pick up on our own. Think about the people that you work or live with. Sometimes you know as soon as they walk in, you pick up on their body language, the tone and intonation of their voice; you might pick up on these cues and decide to go and make them a cup of tea, or stay far away from them for a bit! We have empathy to thank for this, that and how we have learnt to pick up these social cues through responding to and learning from others, but what is going on in our brain for this to happen? Conkbayir (2017), tells us, "neurons are the building blocks of the brain" that send and receive messages by using neurotransmitters that move through the synapse and fire up our neurons, shaping and developing our brains. Mirror neurons quite simply become activated when we see someone doing something, like a movement or action, or observing an emotion – happiness, sadness, fear, or pain. We are wired to learn from one another, and mirror neurons play an important part in early childhood development, but also socially as we grow, live, and work closely together.

Neuropsychology researcher, Stephanie Dimitroff, informs us that we should think of stress positively as it is, "the foundation for empathy, and without emotional contagion, it would be harder to understand what others are experiencing", stress is here for an "evolutionary reason". If we notice that we are experiencing stress contagion personally or professionally, then let us use it for the purpose it is intended, to keep us safe. Are we all just ignoring those signals of stress? Do we allow others to respond and take care of us? We must give ourselves permission to take care of ourselves and each other, as we are biologically wired to do. Let us also reflect upon emotional contagion. I discussed empathy as an EYE superpower in the introduction, and one that likely, none of us has ever been taught about, let alone learnt how to utilise positively in our everyday lives. Emotional intelligence is a life skill that is essential for empaths or those susceptible to experiencing emotional contagion.

KATE'S STORY
When work takes over

I had managed to get some time out of work for my daughter's special Mother's Day assembly, which was, in actual fact, a guilt-ridden hour and a half and every moment that ticked by fuelled my stress levels and exacerbated my sense of panic.

There are other occasions I felt the same; legging it out of work for a Christmas lunch with 163 infants and parents squeezed into a tiny hall, clock watching, eating undercooked sprouts, and jostling for chocolate cracknel before running out of the school hall and back to work with a party hat still on my head.

I will never have these moments back, and I wish I had been more aware of how taking care of my mental health would have provided me with the solutions that I so obviously needed.

These moments, events, concerts, sports days are special moments to cherish, yet I was so busy taking care of other people's children and trying to prove how dedicated I was to the job role that I had not noticed the stress slowly taking over and over spilling into every aspect of my life, spoiling these moments, allowing paranoia and negative thoughts to take over until I was operating in a constant fight or flight mode. I let that stress take over until it was affecting my mental and physical health.

Signs of stress

We all have a uniquely different tolerance to stress, which explains why even those of us who appear to be alike and share similar character or personality traits react, respond to, and experience stress differently. What might be stressful and too much for one person and may lead to mental health issues, may be manageable for another. The way stress can affect us is based upon our vulnerability to stress that is linked to biological, psychological, and social factors (Zubin & Spring, 1977).

How does stress show up?

Stress can affect us physically, emotionally, and behaviourally by paying attention to our bodies, connecting our emotions – thoughts and feelings – with physical sensations in our bodies, and how this influences our actions and behaviour.

The charity Rethink Mental Illness (www.rethink.org) identifies the following signs and symptoms (see Table 2.1).

Table 2.1 Signs and symptoms of stress

Physical	Emotional	Behaviour
Headaches	Worry about future or past	Crying
Sweating	Imagining the worst	Eating more or less
Stomach problems	Being forgetful	Biting your nails
Muscle tension or pain	Not concentrating	Avoiding others
Feeling tired or dizzy	Feeling irritable	Sleep problems
Sexual problems	Racing thoughts	Rushing tasks
Fast heartbeat	Going over and over things in your mind	Drinking or smoking more
Dry mouth	Making mistakes	Being irritable
Short of breath	Feeling low	Being snappy

Sources of stress

Stress can come in many different forms; some examples include:

- **Physical stress** – late nights, binge drinking, illicit drug use, lack of routine, poor diet, illness
- **Environmental stress** – poor housing, social isolation, unemployment,

new environments to adjust to, such as moving to a new house or holidays

- **Emotional stress** – relationship problems, peer pressure, high expressed emotion within the family home, conflicting cultural values and beliefs, leaving home, marriage
- **Acute life events** – bereavements, physical illness/accidents, arrest/ imprisonment, fights, pregnancy and childbirth, rape, and assault
- **Chronic stress** – accommodation problems, debts, prolonged use of drugs/alcohol

Taken from the Adult MHFA Manual (MHFA England, 2016).

When your body is stuck in threat detection system mode, and your brain is still on high alert, you are frozen in your stress response. Just telling yourself that it is okay will not quieten down the message centre in your brain, especially if you are still in an environment that is in any way perceived as threatening. Finding a way to communicate to your body and your brain that you are out of danger will alleviate the surge of hormones and neurochemicals and let your nervous systems, digestive system, immune system, cardiovascular systems know that they are safe (Nagoski & Nagoski, 2020: p. 7).

Burnout and compassion fatigue

Interestingly, just about all research on burnout links to professional burnout, and in particular, those *people who help people* experiencing high levels of stress, with high-pressured standards. Sound like anyone you know or work with? The term "burnout" was developed by Herbert Freudenberger (1975) who studied how burnout is an occupational hazard of the childcare worker (1977). It includes:

- **Emotional exhaustion** – the fatigue that comes for caring too much for too long
- **Depersonalisation** – the depletion of empathy, caring and compassion
- **Decreased sense of accomplishment** – an unconquerable sense of futility: feeling that nothing you do makes a difference

(as cited in *Burnout*, Nagoski & Nagoski, 2020).

According to the Institute for Quality and Efficiency in Health Care (2020), the three main symptoms of burnout are:

• **Exhaustion**: people affected feel drained and emotionally exhausted, unable to cope, tired and down, and do not have enough energy. Physical symptoms include things like pain and gastrointestinal (stomach or bowel) problems.

• **Alienation from (work-related) activities**: people who have burnout find their jobs increasingly stressful and frustrating. They may start being cynical about their working conditions and their colleagues. At the same time, they may increasingly distance themselves emotionally and start feeling numb about their work.

• **Reduced performance**: burnout mainly affects everyday tasks at work, at home or when caring for family members. People with burnout are very negative about their tasks, find it hard to concentrate, are listless, and lack creativity.

Some of these symptoms may look similar to symptoms of depression. However, burnout is thought to be work-related, causing stress, fatigue, and feeling unable to cope. As we have discovered, when these issues are not addressed, they can lead to further physical and mental health issues. Nicholson et al. (2020) note the cultural differences of burnout that may lead to educators experiencing burnout in different ways due to cultural, social supports, or the role of religion.

In EY, we have high expectations and demands for educators, and issues arise when there is little or no level of support in the form of training or professional development, either during the induction or ongoing supervision and appraisal, and this can undermine all of the health and wellbeing benefits that going to work can bring. Burnout can lead to compassion fatigue, which is described as the negative "cost of caring".

Interestingly, the Compassion Fatigue Awareness Project (compassionfatigue.org) indicate the origins of compassion fatigue can begin in childhood, linking to ACEs and the increased risks to our health. Furthermore, the younger we are when faced with caregiver responsibilities, the more we learn to put others' needs before our own. Whilst compassion fatigue is linked to roles that witness ongoing emotional and physical trauma, such as nurses, doctors, and vets, the link to early childhood is nonetheless relevant, especially when we consider our work with children who have experienced trauma, abuse, neglect and our ongoing relationships with vulnerable children, children on child protection registers, adoption. Compassion fatigue is also likened to secondary traumatic stress; when you are working with children who are dealing with trauma, there is a possibility you can experience it too. Again, there is very little consideration in EY of the impact on the development of trauma-informed practice in relation to educators' health and wellbeing. The key to preventing and overcoming burnout is the philosophy of putting wellbeing at the heart and centre of your EY pedagogical approach. Staff who are trained to understand and address stress, know the warning signs of burnout, engage in self-care and respect considerations for staff who will have cultural differences in relation to their health and wellbeing; and for our neurodiverse colleagues and those with a disability, and physical and mental health conditions.

SARAH SCOTLAND, NUTRITIONIST

Does what you are eating affect your mood?

What food we eat can make a significant impact on our stress levels and hence our moods.

When stress takes hold, the body calls for additional support, often in the form of food. Unfortunately, we are often tempted by highly processed foods, high in salt and fats: pizza, biscuits, chips, chocolate, and cake are all examples. The sugar in these foods raises cortisol levels as well as adrenaline. Ultimately, they don't help stress levels or moods. The sugar gets absorbed straight away, giving us a big sugar hit, resulting in a rollercoaster ride when sugar dips and more sugar is craved.

Have a moment to think about the type of foods you eat.

You might be in a rut and eat the same food every day. This is so easy to do – it makes life easy and convenient. However, sometimes the body objects and wants to try something different.

- It is always difficult to remember what we have eaten – so try keeping a simple food diary and write down emotions.

Did these trigger you to eat or reach for that cup of coffee or a specific type of food?

- Water is the best drink in the world. Dehydration can affect mood, but often during the day, we turn to tea and coffee, constantly as a habit, and sometimes to keep you alert. Unfortunately, too many cups of caffeine will give you an artificial high as well as an elevated heart rate.
- Try eating foods that are low in glycemic index (GI), that release sugar more slowly. This enables the body to stay in a steady state. Try porridge, lentils, beans, sourdough bread, wholegrain cereals, and so on.

If you are going to make changes to your diet, then change slowly, do not suddenly bombard your body! If you increase your intake of fruit and vegetables too suddenly, you may find your digestive system gets upset. A sudden cut down on caffeine may give you headaches.

Make small changes and gradually notice the difference. Monitor how you feel. Are you more alert, more aware, less irritable, able to stay up later at night or wake up in the morning not feeling tired?

SHADA'S STORY

Let me give you an example of how sometimes the best intentions, when it comes to wellbeing, can often lead to further stress, frustration, dissatisfaction, and even resentment

My name is Shada Lambert and I am an international career nanny. As nannies, our role is to support families and be a third parent to help the household run smoothly. However, with demanding hours, working as much as 12 to 16 hours a day, it can be a fast-track route to burnout. Working 24-hour days can also take its toll as you become extremely tired and exhausted very quickly. I was booked to work for a family overseas and signed a contract to work 47 hours over six days. When I first started the role, I wanted to impress the family and show them how good of a nanny I was. That's why, when they asked me to work an extra hour or day, I would always say yes, thinking this

was my way of showing I'm dedicated to my career. Instead, it was a recipe for disaster, because all it did was not set boundaries and left me working over 30+ hours extra every week. One day I was working 10 a.m. to 10 p.m. and was asked at 10 p.m. when the parents came home if I could have the baby monitor for the night. Tired and near to exhaustion, I agreed, even though I really wanted to politely decline. It was a new job, and I didn't want to come across as lazy or work shy, so I said yes. It became a regular occurrence for the parents to ask me to do overtime, and each time I would agree. The more regularly they asked, the more resentful I would become for their asking me. I would get angry at myself for not having the courage to say no without feeling guilty. I become so stressed out, dissatisfied with working long hours with one day off a week I became frustrated. On one occasion, I was so exhausted from working a 24-hour shift I woke up so late that I had slept through my alarm. I had forgotten to wake up the children in the morning, and they were late for breakfast. That was a huge wake-up call for me because had I politely declined, I would have woken up on time and been well-rested. When situations like this arise now, I politely decline and offer an alternative at a later date, when I know I will be better rested. Before, I found it very difficult to take a break from work, and I really struggled with saying no. However, now I make sure I schedule days off every few months to avoid exhaustion and burn out. I take pride in setting boundaries, so I don't agree with things I am not happy to do any more.
Shada Lambert/Nanny Sharz

Mental health issues and mental health conditions

As we have learnt, mental health is how we think, feel, behave, and interact, so here we will seek to understand mental health issues and mental health conditions. If we do not know much about a subject or feel unsure about something, like mental health conditions, we might feel scared or worried that we may say the wrong thing and offend someone, so often we choose not to say anything at all. Truly, the only way we can ever get something wrong is by not saying anything at all. You do not need to be an expert; you just need to care.

For example, many of you reading this may feel this way about the subject of mental health and mental ill-health, and this view will have been formed by many things – what we hear in the world around us, the way the media discuss mental ill-health, where we live, and it might be based on personal or family experience or connections, such as religion, ethnicity, culture, and family beliefs. Every one of us will have our personal beliefs that will contribute to our perspective of how we view any given situation.

Part of addressing the stigma and discrimination that exists around mental illness is the language and terminology that we use when talking about mental health and mental illness. Despite mental health being much more widely talked about, stigma still stops people from getting the help they need when they are experiencing mental health issues. I believe we all have a personal responsibility to understand mental health, and distinguish between mental health and ill-health. It is also important here to consider the way that we can self-stigmatise, so often we can be our own harshest critic, we can be unkind to ourselves, get in our own way, and give ourselves a really hard time.

We know one in four people will experience mental health issues over a 12-month period; like any statistics, they are only valid if people are getting support and sadly, we know statistics related to mental health are in fact much higher, as many people are not coming into contact with medical professionals and receiving the help, care, and intervention that they need. Mental health issues such as stress, fatigue, insomnia, anxiety, low mood, if not supported, can lead to mental illness, which are "mental health conditions – disorders that affect your mood, thinking and behaviour", such as "depression, anxiety disorders, eating disorders and addictive behaviours" (World Health Organization, 2014).

Anxiety – the overwhelm of feeling

A certain amount of anxiety is good for us; it spurs us on, helps to get things done, complete tasks, achieve success, and make accomplishments. We have learnt this when exploring stress earlier in the chapter. We will all experience symptoms and feelings of anxiety from time to time, especially when we are trying new things or operating out of our comfort zone. Over our lifetime and as adults, we have also learnt through trial and error that the risk pays off; the reward for trying the new or scary thing is worth it. In the world we live in, the word anxiety is thrown around a lot, so in some ways, we have become complacent about the word and what it truly means. There is a difference between experiencing normal symptoms of anxiety and ongoing anxiety and/or being diagnosed with an anxiety disorder. Anxiety can become problematic when the anxiety we experience starts to become out of proportion with the threat or danger, and starts to impact our daily life, causing a loss of enjoyment and ability to do things that we once enjoyed. There are many different types of anxiety disorders that impact a person's thoughts, feelings and emotions, behaviour, and very real physical symptoms that lead to a person experiencing panic attacks that may feel like a heart attack. More people have anxiety disorders than we might realise, and they are often untreated and under-diagnosed.

Types of anxiety disorder include:

- Generalised anxiety disorder (GAD)
- Panic disorder (attacks of panic or fear)
- Post-traumatic stress disorder (PTSD)
- Social anxiety disorder
- Obsessive-compulsive disorder (OCD)
- Specific phobias (an overwhelming fear of a specific object, place, situation or feeling)

There are various different factors that may contribute to the development of anxiety disorders. Factors may be a combination of biological factors, such as genetics, physical illness, or injury, and psychological or social factors such as trauma or ACEs, socioeconomic background, employment, family and personal relationships, and living or work environment.

ELAINE'S STORY

I worked in a nursery that supported me through my EY degree, which I feel I would never have completed should I have had to pay for it myself, which I will always be forever grateful for. However, within this job (and I only realise it now much later), I was working daily with high functioning anxiety. I constantly worried about what the managers thought and whether I was in trouble. I suffered from quite a few illnesses and would pick up bugs easily from the children; then, when I got ill, I would feel incredibly low. When I was unable to come to work, I would have to go through a process of calling in and speaking to a manager, who would then interrogate me on what my symptoms were and why I wasn't well enough to come in. Often with disbelief, I once called to say my dad had suffered a heart attack. I couldn't repeat what I was met with. I still shudder to think of that conversation and how it affected me after when I was told it shouldn't mean I should be off. This only proved to raise my anxiety and then make me even more worried about how work would be on my return, which was often silent treatment until they felt the need to speak to me again.

Silent treatment continued for many reasons. I was always unsure what I had done. I would try to work to please them, rather than for my own satisfaction and for the sole reason for ensuring the children were well looked after, safe, secure, and having fun. Then there would be times I was spoken to with respect and treated well, and I would think everything would be okay. But I was always waiting, second-guessing why I was ignored one morning, why they had spoken to a colleague so nicely and not me. And it goes on. I stayed in this role as room leader for 14 years. I felt so emotionally attached to this nursery, and because of what they had helped me to do with regards to my degree, I felt indebted.

I went through a lot of family trauma whilst there, my brother taking his own life and then my mother passing away shortly after. It was then I started to really struggle more openly with my anxiety and not coping with high-pressure days at the setting. I remember calling to say the doctor had signed me off because I was suffering from post-traumatic stress disorder, and this was met with a sigh and then okay and the phone being put down. Not only was I going through the worst time in my life, but I felt the guilt and shame of yet letting the nursery down.

When I started to recover, I began to realise that I could not continue any more in this toxic environment. Even my own leadership styles were becoming modelled on what I had experienced myself, and I needed to make a change.

I found a setting, a much smaller one, and was coping really well, the difference in leadership styles was astounding, and I found myself wanting to be there and not wishing a way out of there.

I soon was promoted to manager and absolutely loving how appreciated I was within my setting. My knowledge for working so many years was listened to, appreciated and the way the nursery was managed on a personal level showed me how things really should be.

Unfortunately, my mental health issues reared their ugly head again, as I have now found that stress is a major trigger for me, and oh how I was stressed, constantly dealing with staff shortages and being a small team took its toll, I had a complete breakdown and could not function. What was different in this instance was the owner of the nursery. She was supportive, gave me time and tried to support me wherever she could.

All of this experience has taught me how NOT to be with staff, how to lead with compassion and empathy for what someone else is going through. We also need to find ways to make our working environment a more pleasurable place to be. I have realised that being a leader isn't dictating what you want and having no room for manoeuvre but instead that it is a case of listening to your staff and as you would with the children really noticing when they are struggling and be there to offer support. As ultimately happy and valued staff are what is going to support the children to thrive. Yes, we have to draw the line in some places, but I have found nurturing, talking, and really listening to my team has helped them massively to grow in their practice.

I think the worry always is that if we are not coping, we shouldn't be working with children. The embarrassment is that we need to always be at the top of our game, and that's where burnout really happens.

Elaine Jackson is a nursery manager.

Depression – the absence of feeling

At some point in our lives, we will all face challenges and difficult experiences that lead us to experience the blues. A low mood, sadness, worry, uncertainty, grief, and loneliness. Over time we can bounce back, but when those normal experiences last longer, linger, or do not budge, they can lead to depression. The Mental Health Foundation states depression "causes people to experience low mood, loss of interest or pleasure, feelings of guilt or low self-worth, disturbed sleep or appetite, low energy, and poor concentration". Like anxiety, risk factors for depression include genetics, physical illness or injury, and a combination of psychological and social factors.

According to the Diagnostic and Statistical Manual of Mental Disorders, fifth edition (DSM-5) criteria, the two core symptoms of depression are:

- During the last month, have you often been bothered by feeling down, depressed, or hopeless?
- Do you have little interest or pleasure in doing things?

If two "core" symptoms have been present most days, most of the time, for at least two weeks, ask about:
Associated symptoms of depression:

- Disturbed sleep (decrease or increase compared to normal)
- Decreased or increased appetite and/or weight
- Fatigue/loss of energy
- Agitation or slowing of movements
- Poor concentration or indecisiveness
- Feelings of worthlessness or excessive or inappropriate guilt
- Suicidal thoughts or acts

 KERRY'S STORY

I certainly like to appear as though I have it all together especially in my career. It is the one domain in my life that has given me relative

stability and success. But in truth, my depression is a very dominant part of my identity. Suffering from depression and working with
children can trigger some very conflicting feelings. I want to initiate
authentic connections with the children I care for, but I also must
decide how much of my depression I swallow down.

Like many others, my initial decision to work in the early years is
based on my own early childhood experiences. I faced a lot of trauma
and adversity, and I did not want other children to go through what
I went through. It took years of therapy to recognise that we cannot
repair our pasts through other children, and so I have worked hard to
be a positive influence, but to understand the boundaries of caregiving.

At 24, I was the room leader for a large pre-school, a job I loved but
struggled to do. At the time, I was dealing with a lot of issues. I was
overwhelmed with despair and many things felt beyond my control.
My job, however, really kept me going. No matter how debilitating
my feelings were, I found a way to get up every day, smiled, welcomed children and families, worked alongside, and laughed with
colleagues, and maintained the standard of my work to the best of my
ability. I strived to be "good enough" because that is all I could offer
at the time and now it is my mantra for life.

One day while speaking to a colleague, she caught me at a particularly vulnerable moment at lunch, and I shared with her that
I suffered from depression. She looked quizzical and said, "Well
you don't look depressed, you were laughing earlier on". I was
stunned. Facing your depression is like wading through mud and so
when you get to the other side of a day and that is belittled or even
questioned, it is like a punch in the gut (and you fall face first back
into the mud).

On reflection though, my depression has never been taken that
seriously because I do not really "look" depressed, plus I rely on
funny anecdotes and humour to avoid the intimacy of mental health
discussions. Depression, for me, is a profoundly private experience
and so the signs and symptoms are often dealt with away from the
workplace.

Since that particularly horrific period, I have met many colleagues
with depression and anxiety, and what never fails to surprise me
is that everyone's depression looks different and is dealt with in

different ways. The common thread, however, is that they have all learned to adapt to their depression because it is not something you have, it is something you live with. It takes a huge amount of courage to get through each day and to still be standing but to outsiders, that battle is just not always visible. Just because someone does not "look" depressed, it does not mean that they are not feeling it.

Kerry Payne is a lecturer; EY SEND specialist and author. @eyfs4me

Depression and anxiety, coexisting together

How can the overwhelm of feeling coexist with the absence of feeling?

We know that anxiety and depression coexist, and often people do not understand how the absence of feeling – depression – and the overwhelm of feeling – anxiety – can exist together. Think about how anxiety slowly begins to make your life and the world gradually smaller, and we begin to limit our daily actions; over time this leads to a lack of enjoyment, a decrease in our levels of satisfaction, less connection with others, which can lead to a feeling of low mood and eventually depression.

Brain chemistry

Many people may have an understanding that a chemical imbalance within the brain can lead to symptoms of low mood and cause depression. Serotonin is a neurotransmitter and responsible for almost all of our brain functioning; acting as a messenger for our nervous system, it regulates our mood, such as our feeling of happiness that contributes to our overall wellbeing and can also affect our sleep, memory, attention, appetite, and digestion (Berger et al., 2009). Dysregulation of serotonin is known to be a link to the development of mental health conditions such as anxiety and depression. Medication used to treat anxiety and depression is most commonly selective serotonin reuptake inhibitors (SSRIs), which increase serotonin levels and improve symptoms. Interestingly, despite serotonin being a neurochemical, it is produced outside of the brain; in fact, 90% of the serotonin is produced in our gut (Carpenter, 2012) and the effects of gut health on human health is an area of interest in neuroscience as it links the health of our gut to our mood. A poor diet is then to be considered as a risk factor for depression (Evrensel & Ceylan, 2015).

Because stigma exists around mental health, there is still a stigma around taking medication for mental health issues; especially so, when you work with children. This may come from outside influences from family, friends and what has shaped our opinions on antidepressants, which may mean that people may be reluctant to take or admit to taking them. Medication is not for everyone, but it's unfortunate if people are put off from taking them when they could be one part, even a small, short-term part, of recovery. For others, medication might always be something that helps them to function. The more we talk about this, the more it normalises conversations about recovery, giving autonomy and control to people – such as your friends, family, and colleagues who are taking medication or who may consider it in the future.

It is important to point out that medication alone does not mean cure, that taking medication is just one step to feeling well, and there will be a whole combination of things that an individual will be trying. Such as

- Nutrition
- Exercise
- Yoga and mindfulness
- Spirituality
- Faith, religious beliefs
- Self-help books
- Talking therapies include cognitive behavioural therapy (CBT), counselling, other therapies, and guided self-help
- Community groups
- Alternative therapies, acupuncture, and reflexology

Medication

KATE'S STORY

I started taking diazepam to help with the panic attacks that had started happening more regularly but were still very much occasionally, as and when. However, when these became a permanent state, I can't even describe how much physical pain I was in. The physical symptoms of anxiety had such a grip on me. It felt like my head was on fire. The pain in my chest felt like a permanent weight around my neck, and it hurt to breathe. Hearing a loud noise or being surprised by something unexpectedly could send me into a panic. Hot intense flushes across my body. I constantly needed the toilet, even at night and waking in the night in the grip of terror, and dreaded panic, and then sometimes from nowhere waking in the morning to the very familiar but unwelcome feeling of anxiety, being back threatening and present. My emotions were all over the place. I started to take beta-blockers to help with the anxiety and sertraline for depression. I saw my doctor once a week, and each week I walked in, she would say, "how can I help you today", which was soul-destroying each week, reminding her of why I was there. My dosage kept being increased. I went from running half marathons and being very sociable, to being housebound. But the medication took away the hurt; it was a relief to not have to fight the physical pain for a while. My family did not want me to take medication. It was frustrating having to explain myself. It helped me considerably, and I do not think I would have got through it if I had not had the medication. There also came a time when medication had halted my recovery. I had gained a lot of weight and was really suffering from a chest infection and pleurisy, and when I was told I was obese, and that a side effect of the medication might be contributing to pleurisy and breathlessness, I decided to slowly come off the medication. I went from feeling numb and nothing to feeling everything! Medication had been one small part of my recovery. There were and are so many other things that I had discovered about myself that I needed as the basics to feel healthy and well. I continued to take diazepam for the panic attacks that I experienced less frequently, but still show up from time to time. But more recently, my mental health was starting to decline again, and I was finding everyday tasks such a struggle. How I thought and felt about myself was became noticeably different. This time I managed to have a conversation with a doctor who was really helpful; he listened, we talked through a range of medication, and I have started taking a low dose of citalopram that, along with all of the other things I do to take care of myself, has contributed to me feeling back to myself again.

A few things that I have learnt about support from the GP and medication

- Ask at your surgery which GP has the most interest or specialist knowledge in mental health and would be the best person to speak to
- Ask for a full health check, ask for blood tests to eliminate low vitamin D or any other factors that might be affecting your mental health
- Ask for a telephone appointment if you cannot get to the doctors
- Refer yourself for IAPT (Improving Access to Psychological Therapies) services. They offer talking therapies, such as cognitive behavioural therapy (CBT), counselling, other therapies, and guided self-help and help for common mental health problems, like anxiety and depression www.nhs.uk/service-search/find-a-psychological-therapies-service/
- Find out what support is available within your workplace. Do you have an employee assistance program (EAP) where you can access free and confidential counselling?
- Visit Able Futures, support for mental health at work: https://able-futures.co.uk/

Support

More people experience mental health issues than we might realise, and over our lifetime, we will all experience some form of mental health issues depending on what and for how long we are dealing with something. If you are feeling this way, it is important you know that there is help, support, and treatment available. You are not alone in feeling this way. How well we are able to access help, support, and care is essential because the earlier the intervention, the less likely we are to reach illness, become more unwell and/or receive a diagnosis. When we focus on our health from the starting point of wellbeing, then we might find conversations around mental health in our workplaces becoming normalised. Likewise, if we are trained in mental health first aid, we can learn to spot signs and symptoms that lead to early intervention and signposting.

Care

I have seen settings state they have risk assessments in place for staff who are taking antidepressants, which seems like another way to shame someone to me. If we come from a starting point of compassion and care, staff will learn to trust that we will do the right thing by them. We want to ensure we are doing all we can to support them within the workplace and that they have all they need in order to fulfil their job role and responsibilities. Then, we are also able to address any other issues that may arise and make reasonable adjustments. We all win when we create mentally healthy workplace cultures, whereby staff are able to open up to line managers because they trust they will do right by them, have systems in place that support and enable them to do their jobs, free from discrimination.

A word on language

The language and terminology that we use in everyday life is important, as the way we talk about ourselves and other people, the meaning and value we place on things through the words we use, influences and shapes not only our own perceptions but people around us. When we think about the language that we use about our mental health and mental ill-health, we might find it is limited. It is much easier to talk about mental health negatively than it is positively. Often without realising it, our everyday words, language, sometimes joke language, and self-deprecating humour reinforce negative stereotypes of mental ill-health. When we label ourselves and others as mental, crazy, loopy (insert your own), we are sending messages, however small, that continue to perpetuate the myth that mental ill-health belongs to a certain type of person, undesirable personality trait, or characteristic. Think of it this way, if in our workplaces, our homes and social lives, the people we spend time with openly joke, banter, or ridicule mental health, then if you are feeling low, or if your mental wellbeing has declined, or if you have a diagnosis, this only makes it harder to accept how you might be feeling and makes it harder to open up and talk to others.

I remember seeing a job interview for an early years educator role within a nursery, and within the text, it said something along the lines of mood hoovers, Debbie downers, lemon suckers, drains, need not apply. What do you think of this? If you read this, what would you think? I read it and thought, well, straight away, I know this is not an organisation I would want to work for. It perpetuates judgement, labelling, and reinforces negative judgements and assumptions, none of which is healthy or helpful. As educators, we care for all children; we get to know their personalities, their characteristics, things they like and enjoy; as key workers and as childminders, when we have often much closer and personable relationships with children and families, we get to know children so well. We know the confident, willing to take a risk-children, jump in with both feet, taking charge of the role-play children, that need little encouragement from us. We also know those children who need our hand to hold, they need us side by side for a little longer to encourage, to scaffold, and facilitate interactions with others. We respect them all as unique children. When these children grow up and leave us and go out into the big wide world, their personalities will not drastically change, so why do they have a lack of respect for different characteristics and personalities as adults? To make a team, we need the louder, more gregarious characters as well as the more introverted personalities. When we label each other as mood hoovers and Debbie downers, we are saying, if you are unhappy or have stuff going on, we do not want to hear about it. We are sending and reinforcing messages about toxic positivity. When we demand happiness from each other all of the time, toxic positivity starts to spread and grow. In EY, when we work the hours that we do, day in and day out, we deserve and owe it to ourselves and the children that we care for to work with people who genuinely care about us. Who do not want or force us to leave our problems at the door, who make space so that we can bring all of who we are to work, so that together we can develop our own strategies that enable us to restart our day, lead with health and wellbeing and do a job that we love? When wellbeing is at the heart of all we do, then when issues do arise in the workplace, as they no doubt will, we have the compassion and resources in our toolkits to deal with them in an open, honest, and transparent way that cultivates trust, respect, and dignity.

> Before I went back to work after my second baby, I looked at other jobs, and one nursery was brand new and just opening. I went to look round, and one of the things they talked about was having a 'smile policy' but not in the mental health SMILE terminology, but in the 'when you are at work, we do not want to see any staff being anything other than happy'. This had more of an impact on me, not even wanting to apply than I thought it would have. Who wants to be somewhere where you have to be smiling all the time – I have two children (a newborn at this point), and there were times I wanted to do anything but smile.
>
> Stacey Bilston, Early Years Educator

Supporting someone who does not want help

I often get asked the same question, which is how you can help someone if they do not want help? The honest answer is, you cannot. You are quite far into this book now, so we are unpicking a lot of a lived experience as we make our way through this section; what you have probably been reflecting on is how different someone's lived experience might have been from your own, so there may be many different complex reasons why someone may not want your well-intentioned support. So, no matter how much we have learned or are learning, just because you are ready to listen does not mean someone is ready to talk. Claire Robinson, nursery owner and coach, said to me once, "you cannot see the picture when you are in the frame". I have repeated this sentence so many times because it sums up perfectly how sometimes when we are in the midst of something, we might not have realised just how much it has been bothering or affecting us because we are still stuck in it and dealing with it. It is only later that we can look back retrospectively and recognise just how much we were not ourselves at that time, and only because *now* we identify that we may feel so much better.

How to listen

The best way you can support colleagues, friends, and family is by letting them know you care, and if now is not a good time to talk, then you are always ready to listen. Josh Connelly tells us, "it takes strength to talk, but it takes strength to listen and to hold a space with someone". In EY, we naturally want to fix, solve, and find solutions, so some of us may have the tendency to give unnecessary advice. Can you think of a time when someone gave you some unwanted necessary advice? How did it feel? Possibly like you were being patronised but also like this person was not really listening to you; so in the end, it makes you want to stop speaking. The truth is, rarely can our responses make something better, so all we really have is the here and now, the chance to hold and sit in that space and truly listen to understand, instead of listening to respond.

In the Samaritans' book, *How to Listen* (2021) they share how Samaritans' volunteers seek to listen and understand. As we have said, you do not have to be an expert to help someone who is experiencing a difficult time; listening can help someone work through what is going on and make sense of how they feel. They provide us with SHUSH listening tips.

S – Show you care
H – Have patience
U – Use open questions
S – Say it back
H – Have courage

In our workplaces, the more we put wellbeing at the heart of our practice, the more we are living, breathing, and advocating that health comes first and we genuinely care. The *Thriving at Work* (2017) report by Stevenson and Farmer published a framework of core standards for employers. The core standards are devised to support employers to enhance the mental health of their workplace and empower individuals with mental health conditions to thrive. When we come from that ethos of health; when it is a core value and daily belief, you just may find that this can begin to address the topic of mental health at work too. I passionately believe that we should all have to complete mental health first aid in the same way we complete physical first aid. So that we all have mental health awareness, the knowledge that gives us permission to do a few immediate things, take care of ourselves, be aware of how to look out for others and increase our mental health literacy so that we can reduce the stigma around mental health issues. The more of us that are trained so that we can spot the signs and symptoms and the earlier we get help, support, care and intervention, the less unwell we may become.

Spotting the signs and symptoms

Change in a person is key, so is knowing a person really well

It is easier to spot emotional changes in a person, but with training and in time, we can notice physical and behavioural changes.

- **Emotional**: tearfulness, emotional, irrational, irritated, angry, fear, worry, uncertainty
- **Physical**: change in appearance, unkempt, unhealthy, weight loss/gain
- **Behavioural**: cancelling, rearranging, avoiding, withdrawal, lack of motivation, concentration, forgetfulness, talking less

Workplaces

- Absenteeism/presenteeism
- Reduced productivity
- Loss of morale
- Timekeeping
- Overworking
- Missing deadlines
- Conduct issues
- Lack of cooperation

Suicide

Nobody wants to talk about suicide; it makes us feel uncomfortable, especially if we have a personal connection or experience of suicide; it is emotive and may even be traumatic. We may have also been taught not to speak about suicide because it may give people ideas they did not already have. This is not true. All of the evidence tells us that it is good to talk openly about suicide. Suicide is complex and rarely caused by one thing.

> While the link between suicide and mental disorders (in particular, depression and alcohol use disorders) is well established, many suicides happen impulsively in moments of crisis. Further risk factors include experience of loss, loneliness, discrimination, a relationship break-up, financial problems, chronic pain and illness, violence, abuse, and conflict or other humanitarian emergencies. The strongest risk factor for suicide is a previous suicide attempt.
>
> (WHO, 2021)

In the same way, we are trained to think the unthinkable regarding child protection in safeguarding training. We can apply this logic to suicide; thinking the unthinkable and not presuming anyone is immune because of how they appear or present. Instead, we can use the risk factors we explored earlier in the chapter to allow us to build a picture and consider what might be happening for a person and what they might be dealing with. Thinking, *What is going on for this person, what are they dealing with, how long have they been dealing with it?* The more protective factors a person may have in their lives, the less vulnerable they may be to the risk factors that are present.

Just because a person is having suicidal thoughts does not mean they will act on them. It is more common than you might realise to have suicidal thoughts. "Suicide became conceptualised as a process or a continuum of ideations/behaviours developing from mild to more severe forms of suicidality, most often including the following stages: suicidal ideation, suicide plan, suicide attempt, and completed suicide" (Svetic & De Leo, 2012).

Whilst suicide is a statistically uncommon event, for each completed suicide we know 20 times more people attempt suicide. The human and economic costs are substantial. Suicide is preventable, and we can all play a part, starting with our own understanding, increasing mental health literacy, that can reduce the shame, stigma, and misconceptions that exist around suicide.

WAYS TO GET HELP

Samaritans
You can get free, confidential support at any time by calling the 24-hour listening service on 116 123 or emailing jo@samaritans.org. The number won't show up on your bill. Visit www.samaritans.org for online chat and self-help guidance.

HopeLine UK
0800 068 4141 www.papyrus-uk.org
   For practical advice on suicide prevention:
   Applied Suicide Intervention Skills Training (ASIST): a skills-building workshop that prepares caregivers to provide suicide first aid interventions.

Shout
Text 85258   www.giveusashout.org/
   Anxious/worried/stressed – get 24/7 help from a crisis volunteer.

Black Minds Matter
To make mental health topics more relevant and accessible for all black people in the U.K.   https://www.blackmindsmatteruk.com/

Sad Girls Club
An online platform and community to bring together young Women of Colour with mental health issues.
https://www.blackmindsmatteruk.com/

LGBT Foundation
A wide range of support services; working with healthcare and other professionals to help make public services more accessible and inclusive for LGBT communities. 0345 3 30 30 30 or email helpline@lgbt.foundation   https://lgbt.foundation/

Self-harm is a behaviour and not an illness. Self-harm is very common and affects more people than you might think.

Self-harm usually starts as a way to relieve the build-up of pressure from distressing thoughts and feelings. This might give temporary relief from the emotional pain the person is feeling. It's important to know that this relief is only temporary because the underlying reasons still remain. Soon after, feelings of guilt and shame might follow, which can continue the cycle.

(Mental Health Organisation, 2021)

Eating disorders are not always about weight, they are a way to manage emotions and feelings of distress. "Focusing on food can be a way of hiding these feelings and problems, even from yourself. Eating problems can affect you in lots of ways" (Mind, 2021) Also see:

www.beateatingdisorders.org.uk/support-services/helplines

Psychosis is an umbrella term used to describe a range of conditions such as schizophrenia, bipolar, and post-partum psychosis, whereby a person experiences changes in thinking, perception, mood, and behaviour (Young Minds, 2021).

CREATE YOUR OWN WORKPLACE WELLNESS TOOLKIT

We know that there is often a waiting list for professional help and support unless it is a crisis situation. Collating sources of information of local and national charities and organisations can be useful as a method of early intervention and signposting for support and information.

MHFA England.
https://mhfaengland.org/
Mental health training online and face to face
MHFA Line Managers Resource

Mind.
www.mind.org.uk/workplace/mental-health-at-work/

Able Futures.
https://able-futures.co.uk/

Mental Health Foundation.
www.mentalhealth.org.uk/sites/default/files/how-to-support-mental-health-at-work.pdf

The Hub of Hope is a first of its kind national mental health database, which brings together organisations and charities, large and small, from across the country that offer mental health advice and support together in one place. Pop in your postcode, or switch on location services, and you can find organisations local to you. https://hubofhope.co.uk/

Five ways to wellbeing. Foresight's Mental capital and wellbeing project considered how to improve everyone's mental capital and mental wellbeing through life.
   Evidence suggests that a small improvement in wellbeing can help to decrease some mental health problems and also help people to flourish. This document, produced by the New Economics Foundation (NEF) on behalf of Foresight, sets out five actions to improve personal wellbeing:

* Connect
* Be active
* Take notice
* Keep learning
* Give

www.gov.uk/government/publications/five-ways-to-mental-wellbeing

Action for Happiness. Their vision is a happier world, with fewer people suffering from mental health problems and more people feeling good, functioning well, and helping others.
   www.actionforhappiness.org/

References

ACE Study. Felitti, V.J., Anda, R.F., Nordenberg, D., Williamson, D.F., Spitz, A.M., Edwards, V., Koss, M.P., Marks J.S. (1998). Relationship of Childhood Abuse and Household Dysfunction to Many of the Leading Causes of Death in Adults, 14(4), 245–258. Available at: https://www.ajpmonline.org/article/S0749-3797(98)00017-8/fulltext

Berger, M., Gray, J.A., & Roth, B.L. (2009). The expanded biology of serotonin. *Annual Review of Medicine*, 60, 355–366. [online] https://doi.org/10.1146/annurev.med.60.042307.110802

Block, P., & Burnett Heyes, S. (2020). Sharing the load: Contagion and tolerance of mood in social networks. *Emotion*. [online] https://doi.org/10.1037/emo0000952

Breit, S., Kupferberg, A., Rogler, G., & Hasler, G. (2018). Vagus nerve as modulator of the brain–gut axis in psychiatric and inflammatory disorders. *Frontiers in Psychiatry*, 9. Available at: www.frontiersin.org/article/10.3389/fpsyt.2018.00044

Buchanan, T., Bagley, S., Stansfield, R., & Preston, S. (2011). The empathic, physiological resonance of stress. *Social Neuroscience*, 191–201. [online] doi: 10.1080/17470919.2011.588723.

Carpenter, S. (2012). That gut feeling. *Monitor on Psychology*, 43(8). Available at: www.apa.org/monitor/2012/09/gut-feeling

Chaput J.P. (2010). Short sleep duration promoting overconsumption of food: A reward-driven eating behavior? *Sleep*, 33(9), 1135–1136. [online] doi: 10.1093/sleep/33.9.1135

Colombus, K. (2021). *How to Listen: Tools for opening up conversations when it matters most*. Samaritans.

Conkbayir, M. (2017). *Early Childhood and Neuroscience: Theory, Research and Implications for Practice*, Bloomsbury.

Dimitroff, S.J., Kardan, O., Necka, E.A., Decety, J., Berman, M.G., Norman, G.J. Physiological dynamics of stress contagion. *Sci Rep*. (2017, July 21), 7(1): 6168. [online] doi: 10.1038/s41598-017-05811-1.

Evrensel A., & Ceylan M.E. (2015). The gut-brain axis: The missing link in depression. *Clinical Psychopharmacology and Neuroscience*.

(2015, December 31), 13(3), 239–44. [online] doi: 10.9758/cpn.2015.13.3.239. PMID: 26598580; PMCID: PMC4662178

Freudenberger, H.J. (1975). The staff burn-out syndrome in alternative institutions. *Psychotherapy Theory, Research & Practice*, 12(1), 73–82. Available at: https://doi.org/10.1037/h0086411

Freudenberger, H.J. (1977). Burn-out: occupational hazard of the childcare worker. *Child Care Q*, 6:90–99. [online] doi:10.1007/BF01554695

Geiker, N.R.W., Astrup, A., Hjorth, M.F., Sjodin A., Pijls, L., & Markus, R.C. Does stress influence sleep patterns, food intake, weight gain, abdominal obesity and weight loss interventions and vice versa? (2017). [online] doi.org/10.1111/obr.12603

Gorvett, Z. (2020). What we can learn from 'untranslatable' illnesses. Available at: www.bbc.com/future/article/20200604-what-we-can-learn-from-untranslatable-illnesses

Hanley, J.H. (1999). Beyond the tip of the iceberg: Five stages toward cultural competence. Available at: https://pdkmembers.org/members_online/academy/L08-BeyondtheTipOftheIceberg.pdf

Institute for Quality and Efficiency in Health Care (IQWiG). Depression: What is burnout? Updated June 18, 2020. Available at: https://www.ncbi.nlm.nih.gov/books/NBK279286/

Malbert, C.H., Picq, C., Divoux, J.L,. Henry, C., & Horowitz, M. (2017). Obesity-Associated alterations in glucose metabolism are reversed by chronic bilateral stimulation of the abdominal vagus nerve. *Diabetes*. (2017),66(4): 848–857. [online] doi: 10.2337/db16–0847. Epub 2017 Jan 12. PMID: 28082456

Mental Health Foundation. (2021). Prevention. www.mentalhealth.org.uk/our-work/prevention

Mental Health Foundation. (2021). The truth about self harm. www.mentalhealth.org.uk/publications/truth-about-self-harm

MHFA England (2016). Adult MHFA Manual.

MHFA Line Managers Resource. Available at: https://mhfastorage.blob.core.windows.net/mhfastoragecontainer/bbaee8ce4864ea11a811000d3ab82d69/Line%20Managers%20Resource%20Screen.pdf?sv=2015-07-08&sr=b&sig=q1c

zB8AI9IEdbWIikuW73vn9uqMGNqFhKILmPki7V4g%3D
&se=2022-02-14T16%3A00%3A44Z&sp=r

Mind. (2021). Psychosis. https://www.mind.org.uk/information-support/
types-of-mental-health-problems/psychosis/about-psychosis/

Nagoski, E. and Nagoski, A. (2020). *Burnout: The Secret to Unlocking
the Stress Cycle*. New York: Ballantine Books.

Nicholson, J., Priya S.D., Julie K., Doménica M., LaWanda W. (2019).
*Culturally Responsive Self-Care Practices for Early Childhood
Educators*. Routledge.

Perry, Bruce, D. Maia Szalavitz. (2011). *Born for Love: Why Empathy Is
Essential – and Endangered*. William Morrow.

Perry, Bruce, Oprah Winfrey (2021). *What Happened to You?:
Conversations on Trauma, Resilience, and Healing*. Melcher Media.

Stevenson, D., Farmer, P. (2017). *Thriving at Work*. https://assets.publishing.
service.gov.uk/government/uploads/system/uploads/attachment_
data/file/658145/thriving-at-work-stevenson-farmer-review.pdf

Sveticic, J. & De Leo, D. (2012). The hypothesis of a continuum in
suicidality: A discussion on its validity and practical implications.
Mental Illness. 4. [online] doi.org/10.4081/mi.2012.e15

Trauma Transformed. https://traumatransformed.org/

Van Der Kolk, B. (2015). *The Body Keeps the Score: Mind, Brain and
Body in the Transformation of Trauma*. Penguin.

WHO. (2021). www.who.int/news-room/fact-sheets/detail/suicide

WHO (2018). https://www.who.int/news-room/fact-sheets/detail/mental-
health-strengthening-our-response

Weale, S. (2021). Teenagers can 'catch' moods from friends, study finds.
www.theguardian.com/society/2021/jan/20/teenagers-can-
catch-moods-from-friends-study-finds

Young Minds. (2018). Addressing adversity. www.youngminds.org.uk/
media/cmtffcce/ym-addressing-adversity-book-web-2.pdf

Young Minds. (2021). A guide for young people. www.youngminds.
org.uk/young-person/mental-health-conditions/psychosis/

Zubin, J., & Spring, B. (1977). Vulnerability: A new view of
schizophrenia. *Journal of Abnormal Psychology*, 86(2), 103–126.
[online] doi.org/10.1037/0021-843X.86.2.103

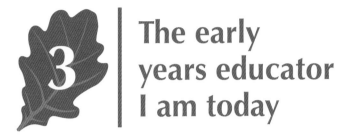

The early
years educator
I am today

When we see people showing up as all of who they are, confident, and shining their light. Let us not be threatened by their shine. Instead, wonder what this person has gone through to be that person I see today?
Kate Moxley

Let your heart and passion guide your work

This chapter will allow us to take some time to reflect upon and consider what has shaped your practice, pedagogy, and beliefs systems. Making space for personal self-reflection on the experiences in your life, both personally and professionally, that have shaped the EYE that you are today. We will consider how our life experiences, education, qualifications, training, professional development, job history, and experiences have moulded and formed our EY values and continuously develop our skills, strengths, talents.

What is *your why*? In the book, *Start with Why*, Simon Senek (2011) tells us that those who know their "why" are the ones that are leading and inspiring others. Starting with the why is a way to think from the inside out, and let your heart and passion guide your work. What is your why? There is an old saying in EY that says, "you are only as good as the setting that you work in", but why have you chosen to

DOI: 10.4324/9781003146247-5

work in the role that you do, in the place that you do it? Greg Bottrill (2018) inspires us to remember the magic of early childhood. He invites us all into the world of good things so that you can "grow your own practice and personal understanding", which helps us to develop our unique beliefs systems of early childhood, which inform our practice that inspires everyday actions and shapes our why.

We cannot pour from an empty cup

True story. When you ask early years educators what they do to take care of themselves, there is usually silence before laughter. Then the famous four-lettered word, an EYE worst nightmare. TIME. We never, ever have enough of it! At home or at work, so we have to use it wisely. We have to create a coalition of care that demands and expects change, from ourselves, from each other, for ourselves, for each other, because of the children that we care for. For this book, I have had the pleasure of having conversations with many different early years professionals. When talking to Joss Cambridge-Simmons about his contribution to this book, he said, "you can't give children the best, when you don't give the best to yourself"; he was resolute in his desire to be "the best man, for himself", if we want to belong in a community that cares, we have to start with self-care. When we enter the EY profession, we understand working with children is rewarding and enjoyable, but we must also understand it can also be stressful and demanding, and taking care of our health and wellbeing and practising self-care is just as vital to us as the qualifications that we seek to gain.

 WHAT IS YOUR EARLY YEARS WHY?

"I can't give you the best of me and leave myself with zero, that's not happening" Joss Cambridge-Simmons

You say you have to be the "best man for yourself, before anyone else"? Tell us about what that belief means to you and how it translates into your practice?

For me, it is my concept of doing for others as I do for myself, is something I call pouring from a cup, so I cannot pour into anyone else's cup if I can't pour in mine first. I've learned that over the years, to be able to give my best to children in my care, I need to be able to be the best version of myself because I can't give you the best of me and leave myself with zero, that's not happening. It's like relationships in general, with your work, with your friends and partners, like it all starts with you, and my dad always told me that the best relationship I'm ever gonna have is with myself – this why I am so great at what I do. I mirror my actions towards myself and the children in my care. I have to live up to me for me. Role modelling the best habits for me, by me, then for others. This enables me to give myself to these families, children, friends, family, and myself, the best Joss.

Joss is the owner and founder of Jossy Care @jossycare

Where you work and the stage you are at in your EY career today will have been influenced by a range of different factors. Woven throughout this book is the way in which we think of our ecosystems, the environments that have shaped our life's course. The EY settings that we have worked, trained, and volunteered in along the way will have significantly imprinted and influenced us in both positive and negative ways. Some of us may be very aware of our lived work experiences that have positively impacted our practice. Likewise, there will also be occasions where we have had to learn from difficult and challenging circumstances.

I returned to employment when my daughter was three. I felt like I was really out of the EY loop, and so I applied for a deputy position within a charity-run PVI setting, covering maternity leave. This job was to teach me many things, but they came through a challenging work experience that forever shaped my practice. My role was based in the pre-school room, but as with most managers and deputies, I would open up the nursery one week and close the next. This meant that there would be regular occasions where I would be in sole charge. One such occasion came about when the manager was not in for a period of time.

When I started this job role, I had informed the management team that my paediatric first aid was out of date. This was back in the days of only needing one named first aider. But I had asked if I could complete it, as there were occasions when I was alone and in sole charge without the manager. I was told no, that I could not. I offered to pay myself out of my own money and again was told no and that I could not have the time out of work to complete it. As I was only maternity cover, they considered it not financially viable, especially as they were a charity. When a child cut their head open in the back garden on a fence, I was in sole charge and had to apply emergency first aid. When applying first aid, it was immediately visible that the cut was down to their skull, and I had to quickly call for an ambulance, and also inform the child's mother. I did what any of us would automatically do to take care of that child in an emergency. It was only afterwards that I realised I had put myself at risk to administer this first aid. If something had gone wrong, I would have been personally responsible for that child's health. I would like to reassure you that the child in question recovered quickly and was soon back in nursery running and racing around with the same enthusiasm and energy.

All these years later, what I know to be true is that I would never again work for an organisation that did not value my professional development, an organisation that would fail to recognise the potential harm and detrimental impact it could have had on children's health and wellbeing. It would lead me to better consider the organisation to which I am applying for a job – why do I wish to work there, do our views, practice, principles, and ethos align? From that day forward, my practice also changed; when in the garden, for example, I became a monitor, constantly on the lookout for any threats or danger. I was what I jokingly describe as the fun police, risk assessing at every opportunity. It was a long time before I was able to feel at ease when working outside.

When experiences like this happen, we can wish that we had never lived them, but if I said I wished I had not taken that job opportunity, then I would not have had the breadth of experience I have today. This job role enabled me to work with staff, children, and families and learn about different cultures, family values, and beliefs that I had not had the pleasure to work with so closely before. It broadened my professional development and developed my personal development to see a different view of the world from my own.

Do you have any similar incidents to describe?

What has shaped and formed your work ethics?

This activity will enable you to look at different aspects of your career and work experience, from education, training, professional development, job history, significant or noteworthy events or experiences; colleagues, managers or those who have left a lasting imprint; children, and families we have cared for, and how all of these experiences enabled us to form our practice and continuously develop our skills. This activity is broken into two reflections, from your window of the world as your younger self and reflections today.

Using Table 3.1, reflect upon your work experiences and what has shaped and formed your views and beliefs; this can be a helpful and useful exercise. However, it may also be emotive, so please be mindful of when, how, and who you complete this activity with; especially if you have experienced any situations that might be upsetting or traumatic.

Table 3.1 Reflection on my work life experience

Influences	My younger self	Today
Training and qualifications		
Voluntary work/placements		
First job role		
Career history		
Early years work family		
Significant events		
Promotions		
Children or families you have worked with		
Specific job roles or responsibilities		
Performance management		
Job interviews		
Disciplinaries		
Proudest achievement		
Fondest memory		
Something I would like to forget		
My biggest challenge but my biggest reward		
Anything else		

ROB'S STORY
Lessons to be learnt from the playground to the staff room

Many teaching assistants, nursery nurses, and teachers do not speak out against bullying, fearing the repercussions. Following a few years of silence, I am ready to share my experience and, by changing my approach, how I dealt with day-to-day anxieties whilst working within an early years classroom.

I am taken back to the uneasy days, days when I would go into work with a smile. It disguised my true feelings. Often early years educators put the needs of the children before their own.

I put on a brave face when entering the classroom each day, chronic fatigue and anxiety hidden. I feared the criticism that followed when I did not perform to the same exacting standards metered out by the perfectionists I worked with.

The reality is, as someone who has dyspraxia, I was often overwhelmed when given multiple tasks. No allowances or understanding were evident. My colleagues expected me to perform at a pace outside of my processing range. Amongst other skills, I particularly find multitasking difficult.

One specific example of this; I was filing some of the children's work, the class teacher shouted across the classroom, "can you not follow instructions?" I struggle with using a hole punch. I have challenges with hand-eye coordination and have a tremor in my left hand. The result? The holes were not correctly placed. The teacher that I was supporting was angry and shouted at me. I felt bewildered and hurt.

I found myself overthinking situations and putting myself under undue pressure to perfect my work. This, in turn, increased my stress and anxiety levels.

During this time, no one ever doubted my caring ability or approach to children's welfare or my teaching skills. The criticism was often focused on my slowness or inability to handle multi-verbal instructions that went with the admin of the role.

Interactions with colleagues were minimal as I tried to focus on my work, and at times, I felt invisible. If a colleague inquired about my wellbeing, I would assure them that I was fine, when clearly, I was not.

The journey for male practitioners is not an easy road. Especially, if like me, you are not naturally academic. I followed the vocational EY journey, starting off with three years of studying at college. I discovered that the route to school-based education was often blocked by a perceived lack of academic qualifications (a degree) to progress into mainstream education. My vocational-based qualifications were often discounted in favour of older female staff who were returning to work in a part-time role.

My ideas were often dismissed, and I felt this was because I did not have a degree. Many of my ideas were silenced, and I was caught in an anxiety trap. To be taken seriously in the world of education, I had little option but to accept that we have an upside-down education system. All the emphasis is on the importance of high school and university qualifications, so no matter how passionate I was in my care for children's education; without a degree, there were few openings in teaching.

"Actions speak louder than words"

I decided the way forward was to gain a degree. I achieved a Foundation Degree and a BA.

I achieved this with the support of my then employer who had understood my dyspraxia challenges and helped me cope by adapting my workload and providing me with the tools to make my job easier.

I often think that when you have a hidden learning challenge as an adult, people are so quick to judge. If your disability were visual, would this be the case? People often are not empathetic or do not take the time to understand.

Reflecting back on my early career, a lot of the excellent leading practitioners have definitely shown some signs of mental health issues. These people have all of the natural skills required to be a primary carer, but are often lacking the confidence to stand up to others who are judgemental or who bully.

I eventually decided to consult with a psychotherapist, explaining my emotional turmoil. He recommended a course of CBT (cognitive behavioural therapy), and my life turned 180 degrees. I found the strength to stand up and get control of my emotions and started to tell people of my disability because, after all, that is what it is. He gave me the "tools to cope".

Now with the control of my thoughts in check and the strength to stand up to the playground-style of bullying, I am a better person and someone who cares not only for the children in my class but also my fellow workers.

Rob Fox is the founder of Active Childhood UK and currently working as a nanny.

Shining your light

"You're full of miracles and magic, kindness and light, laughter and love. Elbow those imposter thoughts out of the way and let a little more of you through".
Jayne Hardy, 2020

Throughout the training and consultancy that I do now, I have met, worked, and connected with early years educators across the UK, delivering training or via the wonderful medium of social media, and something that always hits and hurts me is the low self-esteem that so many educators appear to experience. I have delivered training sessions where there have been tears when encouraging educators to think about their skills and talents. I now rephrase this question and ask educators to tell me about the skills, strengths, and talents of their colleagues. This mainly evokes a different reaction, one of joy and laughter, especially when teams are very well connected and there is a sense of belongingness. We are so much kinder to others than we are to ourselves. If only we could see ourselves through the eyes of the children that adore us, if only we were taught as children to shine our light and not hide it. To give ourselves and the people around us permission to concentrate on the things we like, love, and respect about ourselves, rather than paying attention to the parts we do not like or want to change.

JAMEL C. CAMPBELL
Bigging up our Early Years selves

What gives me hope is the small changes and small steps I have made. I say small, but they are big steps, but many of us don't get the acknowledgement we deserve. The EY sector is not held in high regard like other education sectors. Do you know how many big things are happening right now for our sector? We need to be screaming it from the rooftops. When we have colleagues nominated for awards, a win for them is a win for us, a win for the sector. Why are we not talking about that more? *We need to uphold and big up our people, uphold our theorists of today, big up our people, ground-breaking stuff is coming through.* We need to big up our people. So much coming from the EY. I want to promote people on the front line. If we promote our unsung heroes, that deserve to bigged up. We need to give people their flowers while they are here. If it is a win for EY, we gotta promote it.

SPACE FOR PERSONAL REFLECTION.
THE EDUCATOR YOU ARE TODAY

How would your colleagues describe you?
A skill you are most proud of?
Biggest strength?
What training and professional development have you completed recently?
Have you stopped to ask yourself why you work where you do? What made you want to work in this setting?

Do you feel happy and safe at work?

Do you feel valued, supported, and listened to?

How are your skills, talents, and strengths identified and shared with others?

Are they supported to gain further skills to develop your practice even further?

How are you able to progress professionally and aspire for your future development and possible career progression?

The power of your thoughts and beliefs

We are taught many things at school, but I still wonder how much of the hard stuff, that I have had to work out and unlearn as an adult, would have just been so much easier had I, in fact, been taught it in my teens. Like the power of my thoughts on beliefs and the significant impact that had on my mental health and emotional wellbeing. Why are we so much kinder to other people than we are to ourselves? I remember reading a book and crying, where for the first time, it powerfully and painfully hit me that the inner dialogue and voice inside my head that I had been listening to for thirty-odd years was vicious and more of an inner critic and a saboteur. I had become a special agent of self-deprecation and skilled in picking out flaws and all the things I did not like about myself. Hearing these words for the first time was a game-changer for me.

Your thoughts are not facts. Do not believe everything that you think.

Something we are not taught is the power of our thoughts and beliefs is tremendous. We are in control of what we think and believe, but sometimes we develop unhelpful thinking patterns that we call thinking distortions that enable us to collect really unhelpful evidence that influences the way we think, feel, and behave and how we think others are thinking, feeling, and behaving towards us. The thing is, we have over 6,000 thoughts a day! Some we like, some we believe, some we do not like, some we forget, and some we run with. Our thoughts influence the way we feel, and when we develop unhelpful thinking patterns that affect and impact our health and happiness, it is important that we can develop helpful strategies to challenge them. There are simple techniques we can use, such as:

- What would I say to my best friend in this situation?
- How will I feel about this in six-months' time?
- What evidence do I have for this?
- I am taking something personally, that is not about me.

Let me tell you about the time that I started a new job role as a teaching assistant (TA) in the afternoons and was managing a wraparound provision in the morning. I worked alongside another TA, who was experienced in the role and had been doing it for some time. They were also completing their BA (hons). One day, after not working together for long, they said to me, "Oh, I am reading this really good book on leadership and management. I thought you might like to borrow it". I remember thinking, they must not think I am particularly good at my job, but then I went into, "Who do they think they are? I have been working in early years longer than them, I have so much experience, why would I need to read this book?" I was hurt and embarrassed. Then actually furious. This pretty much set the tone for our professional relationship. I thought she was too big for her boots and intimidating and that she thought I was not particularly good at my job. A few years later, when I started my foundation degree and started to realise just how little training and professional development I had actually completed over the years, especially any formal leadership or management training, I realised I should have read that book after all!

The truth of it all is that this TA job was new and challenging, and I already felt like I was not good enough and maybe not clever enough. I felt defensive and developed an armour that I did not even know I had, to try and protect myself from the hurt. I had collected some unhelpful negative evidence that assumed I was a terrible TA and held on to it and used it to form some really unhelpful thoughts and beliefs about a situation and a person that were not actually true, which created insecurity and a lack of confidence, none of which was healthy or helpful. I also believe that when you work in EY, over time, we all develop an armour of protection because the job is so mentally, physically, and emotionally exhausting, and somehow there is always a feeling that we could have done more, could have done better. There is often an element of not being or feeling good enough.

When we allow a little time for self-reflection and self-discovery, we can notice what that inner critic has been telling us and often tricking us with and begin to rewrite the script and identify helpful strategies that develop our ability to think and feel positively about ourselves and what skills we have to share.

Can you think of a work experience where you may have jumped to a conclusion or ran with a thought that was actually unhelpful?

Have you worked with someone that you found difficult or made you feel insecure?

How do you feel about it now?

Stop expecting you from other people

When I was working as a manager, I would often find myself feeling frustrated with my team. Why didn't they appear to care about things as much as me? Why didn't they go above and beyond and make things happen the way I did? If they rang in sick, sometimes I would feel annoyed and think, if I can make it into work when I am not feeling well, so can they! I would bring in cakes and sweets for staff meetings, and sometimes I wondered why I bothered. I would take time to write inspiring quotes and print off nice things for the staff room and staff noticeboard. Half the time, it felt like nobody noticed. Over time I gradually began to resent my team for not making as much effort or seemingly being as dedicated to their job role as me. What was I doing wrong as a manager if I could not inspire this motivation from my team?

There is no big revelation here, but what did provide some clarity was when I realised this. To them, it was *just a job*. Do not get me wrong here, they enjoyed their job role, but it was just a job to them. A job that they all did very well, showed up to every day, and did their best, but went home to enjoy the rest of their lives. They had their own things going on, their own interests and circumstances. I look back now and know they were the ones with the right idea! My team was made up of an array of different personalities and characters. I cannot say every single person was the best of friends with each other, but we were like a family, and we all had our roles and our different skills, talents, and strengths.

The problem, though, was that it was – *so much more than just a job for me*. My job role consumed my life. I have already told you about this stage and phase of my life. I describe this period in my life as "eating, sleeping, breathing EY"! I was also studying for my Foundation Degree and eventually my BA (hons), so I never seemed to switch off, and my job role became my life, and there were never enough hours in the day. My role was brand new, and the pressure was enormous – after many deputy roles and temporary manager experiences, this was my first full-time manager's role, and I wanted to prove I was good enough. So, without realising, that is just what I did, I worked myself into the ground proving myself, proving that I was worthy of this manager's role.

I can look back and laugh about it now, but I do wonder what it must have felt like to have me as a manager during this time. I would come in after reading an article or seeing something, and I would be like, "Wow! Take a look at this, isn't this wonderful?" "How about doing something like this?" I can see the look on some of their faces still, "thinking, what on earth is she on about now?" I can remember coming into work struggling to carry a large lamp for one of the rooms – it was massive and did not even suit the space, and it did look ridiculous! I was just so passionate about what I was doing I would pull us in all different directions with my enthusiasm without even realising it. When I had the opportunity to visit Reggio Emilia with the university, I must have actually been so obnoxious with my thirst for sharing the wonderful things I had experienced!

I see so many managers expressing the same frustrations with the same worries and issues with their team. Understand this; stop expecting you from someone else without knowing it – back then, that is why I was always left feeling disappointed. Just because I was going above and beyond, motivated by my own reasons, doing whatever it took, did not mean I should expect that from my team, but I did. Therefore, they would always fall short of my expectations. In turn, I would work harder, take on more, try to get them to do more, but they would not understand my motivation and not value what I was doing. Therefore, they were not

107

appreciative or grateful. I prided myself on being a role model to them, dedicated and passionate and hoped that would inspire their practice. What I learnt is there is nothing more important than our health. The role model they actually needed from me is one that protected them from anything that impacted our wellbeing. In our case, it was proving to everyone else our provision was good enough – so I let us get carried away doing unnecessary things that took up our time and distracted us from what we were there to do.

Working in EY is so emotive – it becomes more than a job if you let it. Working with children is more than a chosen profession. It is a calling. You have the gift, or you do not. It cannot be taught, so it becomes very personal to you, part of who you are. It is then especially hard to not take things personally when things arise professionally in the workplace. It is impossible to not become emotionally invested when you are caring for babies and children, day in and day out and forming relationships with families and working so closely with colleagues. It is like a family, and like all families, we all have our issues, and our relationships with each other can be a little tricky.

If you are a manager and are having issues with your work family, then having some honest conversations with yourself about your motivations and the expectations you have set for yourself and your team is not only important, but I would also say is essential. We spend so much of our time doing our absolute best to understand the children in our care but to be really happy at work, we need to dedicate some of that time to understanding each other.

Whilst having a job is important and a big part of our lives and our identity – there is also more to life than work. If your job role is impacting your health and happiness, something has to change. That change can come when you find that balance between work, rest, and play.

Emotionally intelligent (EI) leadership

"By teaching people to tune in to their emotions with intelligence and to expand their circles of caring, we can transform organizations from the inside out and make a positive difference in our world".

Daniel Goleman, 2021

What is it? And why do we all need it if we do not want just to survive, we want to thrive!

Did you know that EI is equal to, if not sometimes more important than, IQ? Daniel Goleman, author of *Emotional Intelligence: Why It Can Matter More Than IQ* (1996). There are four domains of EI: self-awareness, self-management, social awareness, and relationship management (see Table 3.2). They exist within the twelve EI competencies described as "learned and learnable", helpful for all of us at work or with leadership responsibilities.

 Table 3.2 Four domains of EI

Self-awareness	Self-management	Social awareness	Relationship management
Emotional self-awareness	Emotional self-control Adaptability Achievement orientation Positive outlook	Empathy Organisational awareness	Influence Coach and mentor conflict Management teamwork Inspirational leadership

Empathy

"Forming mutually empathetic relationships that facilitate reaching out to others: when we reach out for support, we may receive empathy, which is incompatible with shame and judgment. We recognise that our most isolating experiences are also the most universal. We recognise that we are not defective or alone in our experiences".

Steve Safigan, 2012

Empathy is feeling with people

In the Power of Vulnerability TED talk by Brené Brown (2012), she references Theresa Wiseman's four defining attributes of empathy:

- to be able to see the world as others see it
- to be non-judgemental

- to understand another person's feelings
- to communicate your understanding of that person's feelings

Brown defines empathy as a skill. Furthermore, Brown explains how "empathy fuels connection, shame drives disconnection". Shame results in fear, blame (of self or others), and disconnection. Empathy is cultivated by courage, compassion, and connection, and is the most powerful antidote to shame.

A global pandemic gave us all permission to feel

I have always thought it impossible to expect people who work so many hours in such small spaces, not to let others know that stuff outside of work may be bothering them. If I give all my caring for others, I hope people I work with care enough about me. This is about showing up at work with all of who we are and then supporting one another to restart the day and find the appropriate tools and techniques to face the day. If we try to keep everything inside, eventually, it will find a way to spill out. If we genuinely care about each other as people and not just as a resource or a number to cover a ratio, we can let down some of the barriers we use to protect and defend ourselves. That vulnerability enables us to connect and create a greater support network authentically – enabling us to stay in a job role that we love and that we are good at. Ultimately, we must understand that through increased EI, we can improve staff wellbeing and the success of our organisation (David, 2016).

When measuring EI behaviour, Marc Brackett describes in his book *Permission to Feel* (2019) how inspiration, respect, and happiness are much higher in the workplace when line managers have strong emotional skills. This impacts on job retention, productivity, and mental health. Furthermore, Brackett describes how we can be an "emotional judge" – *what is wrong with this person*, or an "emotional scientist" – *genuinely caring what is going on for this person* when interpreting and dealing with emotions at work. EI is not always about comfort and kindness. It takes a significant level of awareness to deliver feedback or handle sensitive situations.

Imagine if we all worked in an EY ecosystem where we were all equipped to be emotional scientists?

- Everyone would listen more and judge less
- There would be less stigma and racism
- All emotions would be appreciated, even the negative ones
- Feelings would be seen as strengths not weaknesses
- More people would be their authentic, best selves
- People would leave their workplace thinking, I can't wait to return tomorrow
- We'd see less self-destruction and more self-compassion
- Depression and anxiety rates would be dramatically reduced
- There would be less bullying, a greater sense of belonging, and more harmonious relationships

(Brackett, 2019)

Empower managers to put wellbeing at the heart of their leadership

It is important to reflect on our individual skills and strengths as a leader, and reflect on our personal areas for development. We all have our own individual leadership style, and our life experience so far will have shaped our own unique window on the world. Have you ever considered what has shaped your beliefs and values? Think about your personal characteristics and how they have formed how you manage and lead people.

IN CONVERSATION WITH KIM ESNARD

Emotional intelligent leadership

"Holding out your hand to bring people with you, allow others to put out their hand out to you, and take you with them".
What do I need to do to be able to show up?
Asking ourselves – what is our why? What is our passion?

On what pillars do we stand? Our purpose often arises from experiences in our own life; the obstacles we have encountered and the qualities we develop to overcome them. In just two years, I experienced divorce after 25 years of marriage, a house move, falling seriously ill with COVID-19 for nine months, losing my business, losing several family members to the virus. How have I come out of this stronger, with greater clarity and drive? I can truly say I am equipped to walk through those fires. Whilst enduring, we still have to lead our families, teams etc. I believe in leading with vulnerability. It enables people around us to enjoy the same freedom and at the same time gives credibility to you when you rise from the ashes. For me, I am happiest when I am of service to others, when I can inspire and help them to be the best version of themselves.

Teams depend on their leader to tell them where they are going, how they are going to get there. Our families and teams are more motivated when we, as leaders, articulate our vision along with the goals to achieve it. What do I need to do this? Self-reflection: it helps us to reconnect with our dreams, our vision, our purpose. We must be willing to look within ourselves. It's impossible to see the bigger picture of who we are and where we are if we are constantly on the go with blinkers. Emotionally intelligent leadership (personal, social and emotional (PSE) for leaders) starts with leading ourselves first.

Protecting my energy

During the pandemic, I delivered a webinar and spoke about protecting our minds, emotions, and spirit – the infectious nature of our words, moods, and behaviour – and reminded others that:

- We need to have some 'infection control' with our emotions, words etc.
- To put on our own oxygen masks first – protecting our inner person

- To recognise what causes us to 'catch' and 'spread' the emotions of others. Social media can sometimes be at the heart of this emotional virus

Self-awareness, our ability to recognise our emotions, motivations, and thoughts

While leadership is about setting the vision and purpose, it also has the ability to emotionally connect us with others and inspire people to become a part of the journey. Emotionally intelligent leaders understand their emotions, their triggers, and are able to 'self-regulate' and provide better results for our people. So many of us will have gone through so many changes and challenges and may have had to rebuild ourselves or think about our self-esteem and self-worth.

Burnout

A practitioner's mental health and wellbeing impacts on their capacity to respond to the needs of the children they are caring for. So, securing a strong base is our starting point.

The feelings and emotions that we recognise in ourselves now, we will recognise in others too, including the children and families we want to support.

EY, in my opinion, seems to have the fast-track ticket to burnout. In my experience, it is singularly the worst experience I have ever had as a practitioner. All of the warning signs ignored or, worse still, not acknowledged, as we continue to drive until every last drop of passion, self-care and vision is buried under a raging sea of expectation and "Self-care really is how we take our power back".

Social media is a virus

As an observer, this is one of the areas that I am particularly careful of treading into – a reflection, not a judgement. The behaviours I have sometimes seen cause me great concern around the negative energy that is sometimes shared. I wonder how we can be so bitter to one another and have positive energy for the children we serve?

Kim Esnard Director at the Early Years Collective, Education & Training Lead at TineyCO. Social Media @ChildcareCoach_

References

Botrill, G. (2018). Can I Go and Play Now? *Rethinking the Early Years*. SAGE Publications Ltd

Brackett, M. (2019). *Permission to Feel*. London: Quercus.

Brown, Brené. (2012). Power of Vulnerability. TED talk.

David, S. (2016). *Emotional Agility: Get Unstuck, Embrace Change, and Thrive in Work and Life*. London: Penguin.

Goleman, D. (1996) *Emotional Intelligence: Why It Can Matter More Than IQ*. London: Bloomsbury Publishing.

Hardy, J. (2020). Kind Words for Unkind Days: A guide to surviving and thriving in difficult times. (p. 42). Orion Spring.

Senek, S. (2011). *Start With Why*. London: Penguin.

2 | A philosophy for wellbeing

Introduction

Going to work should boost our self-esteem and enable us to feel a sense of fulfilment and accomplishment, and positively impact our health. Working with children can bring great joy and happiness and is often described as "the best job in the world" and requires skill, patience, understanding, empathy, and compassion.

Yet sadly, if we are not careful, the exact skills being an early years educator requires of us are the ones it can take away. Often, workload and pressures do get in the way, leading to unhealthy behaviours, attitudes, and even toxic workplace cultures.

The reality is there are many things we can do to address these issues that often come back to the same recurring themes. This part of the book builds on your reading and learning from Part 1. The case studies, reflections, and activities you have already completed will be essential to understanding how Part 2 can empower you to identify the wellbeing issues within your EY role and then take actions to resolve and address them.

Part 2 is dedicated to placing wellbeing at the heart of your EY practice through core values that are interconnected to create a philosophy of wellbeing that is the blueprint at the heart of your everyday actions and practice.

Core values

Core values that become embedded at the heart of the practice inform our everyday purpose and cultivate an early years ecosystem that develops:

- A sense of belonging
- A culture of inclusion

DOI: 10.4324/9781003146247-7

- Relationships based on shared values, creating trust, respect, and dignity
- Staff wellbeing integrated into systems and structures
- A clear vision of pedagogy that inspires practice
- High-quality early years environments that improve outcomes for children

Core values are carefully considered to protect and nurture all of the EY community's health and wellbeing from your EYE to babies, children, and their families. They have the potential to develop a culture of inclusion and belonging, and develop:

- **A vision of team togetherness** that is underpinned by leadership, with a clear philosophy, vision, and ethos that informs all the community's actions.
- **A sense of connection and belonging** to a community of inclusion that cultivates trust, respect, and kinship.
- **Health and harmony** cultivating a mentally healthy workplace environment, nurturing and valuing resilience, promoting work-life balance through a community of care.
- **A culture of kindness and accountability** advocating emotionally intelligent practice that develops reciprocity and trust.

Chapters 4, 5, 6, and 7, focus on each core value and show how each of these can be used to act and create culture change.

Wellbeing at the heart

The starting point for all early years settings must be the health and wellbeing of the EYE, as without them, there would be no early years provision. However, this thought is often lost in translation because of the many legal, statutory, and regulatory requirements that require such a focus and emphasis on what children need and the quality of care they receive.

Of course, this is necessary; however, we need to consider another perspective, which is, *what do staff need*? To be in a position to begin to provide children with the highest quality care, we have to start with the very people that will provide that care. When we shift our focus and set our vision to our EYE and what tools they need, this allows us to have a blueprint to work from that guides us towards a shared philosophy of wellbeing that cultivates inclusion and belonging.

When you display your commitment to staff wellbeing within your systems and structures, it shows that you take your staff's health and wellbeing seriously. It showcases that you do not leave staff happiness to chance. It is not a coincidence that staff, children, and families are happy, healthy, and comfortable in this early years environment. Your intentionality is displayed through the individual ethos and unique approach that informs and underpins everyday purpose, practice, and pedagogy. This consideration has to apply to owners and managers themselves and lone workers, such as childminders and nannies. It takes commitment and intentionality to your personal health and wellbeing.

This type of thinking is, in its simplest form, inclusion. Inclusion is creating a space for everyone – yourself, your team, children, families – and all of who they are, so everyone belongs. Your systems and structures incorporate everything that your unique setting or personal approach offers to enable everyone not merely to fulfil job requirements but to thrive and reach their full potential through appropriate support, care, guidance, and training. When you are responsible for leading and managing other people, this relationship has to work both ways. If you are doing all you can to support staff, you will build a reciprocal relationship that takes dedication and commitment from your whole community. It makes leaders accountable and your team accountable too.

Prioritising what contributes to our overall health, happiness, and job satisfaction is a new way of thinking, a new way of doing things, and a new way of wellbeing for you and your team. It is more than professional development; this is an opportunity for you to develop a healthy working environment that promotes individual reflection and a community of teamwork.

Why are core values important?

LAURA AND GARY'S STORY
Hopes & Dreams Childcare Group

"What opportunities do we provide for children?
More importantly, what opportunities do we provide for staff?"

Tell us more about your core values and the meaningful impact they have for all of your community?

Core values are the foundation for so much of what we do. They underpin our culture and ethos and support our approach to staff wellbeing.

Our core values are a framework for how we, both as a business and as individuals, show up through our values and related behaviours. They were developed in conjunction with our teams and are kept under review.

Strategically we use our core values as a decision-making framework; we use them when considering implementing a strategy or a practical measure, e.g. when recruiting, or whether we should set up an under two provision.

Recruitment and retention is underpinned by our core values. We use them to ensure that our staff family consistently display repeatable behaviours that we all follow. They attract like-minded people who have strong foundations on which to build a positive culture and teamwork.

For our staff family our core values allow staff to anticipate how they will be treated or what they can expect if they have an issue. The clarity of expectation is comforting for staff and gives people a secure feeling. It allows everyone to understand what behaviours our staff family expect from them and how they fit in. Staff can also predict how the business will respond in any circumstance. This reduces conflict and tension that may otherwise arise.

I think the main thing for me is that staff trust that we will respond to them. They trust that we will make the best decisions for them.
We are bringing our core values to life:

- Deliver wow, through caring
- Create trust with open and honest communication
- Pursue growth and learning to drive change
- Build a positive team, and family spirit
- Be passionate, determined, and resilient

How do staff views inform your systems and structures?

Our shared values are at the very heart of everything we do and guide our actions and decisions. They are our culture and describe how we behave internally and externally and underpin and guide our long-term strategy. Significantly they shape our reputation and our brand. Everyone within the team is expected to demonstrate these values in their day-to-day behaviour and encourage others to demonstrate them.

Laura and Gary Peirce are the directors of the Hopes & Dreams Childcare Group and have six day nurseries on the Isle of Man.

Understanding our ecosystem

In EY, we are all familiar with Bronfenbrenner's (1960) ecological systems theory in childhood development. Let us take a moment to refresh our memory, depending on how long ago we studied at college or university. In the simplest terms, the view that our social environment influences our human development, the environment in which you grow up, imprints on every aspect of who you are. Thinking back to the breath of life theory from the Blackfoot Nation, we are reminded how essential community is to our health, thinking of the child, or us as the adult being at the heart of our surrounding community.

As we have already discovered, there are many determinants of health; Bronfenbrenner's theory indicates how the far-reaching impact on children's health, wellbeing, and development is affected by political, economic, and cultural factors in our society that affect the ecosystems that we are nestled within. The ecosystem into which we are born is the microsystem, being our immediate environment and will set our life's course. All external factors in the surrounding ecosystems will be directly influenced from the very beginning of our lives. Throughout our lifetime, the environment in which we live grows and will continue to affect health and wellness and our capacity to flourish.

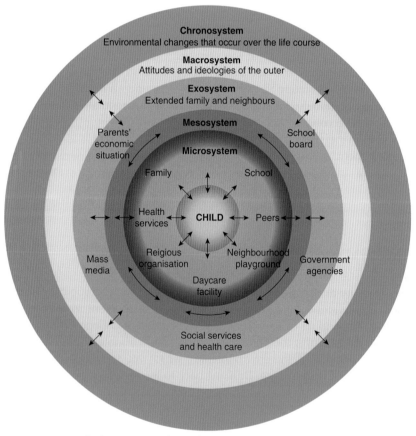

Figure i2.1 Bronfenbrenner's ecological systems theory

As adults, one of our ecosystems becomes our workplace, so the people we work with, the values, beliefs, and attitudes of the people we work with – *our community* – matters; the work we do, the way we do it, the way we are supported to do it. We can use Bronfenbrenner's theory to understand how the working environment influences our wellbeing (Cumming & Wong, 2019): how happy, healthy, and comfortable we are at work and what contributes to that. We can also consider how broader influences within a society affect and influence our ecosystems and the work we do, especially in early childhood, political, and economic factors (MacBlain, 2018). For example, we know funding, early years policy and government initiatives, for instance, all significantly affect us through the ecosystem in which we work, as does the way we are regulated and inspected. When we bring a group of people together to work collectively, as you can see from Figure i2.1, they bring with them all of their life experience, which has developed their attitudes and ideologies to form their values and beliefs. When we show up for work each day, we want to be seen, valued, and respected for all of who we are, and feel as though we belong in the environment in which we work.

Ecosystem, a definition: *all the living things in an area and the way they affect each other and the environment.* (Cambridge Dictionary)

Early years ecosystem

Let us think about how our early years ecosystem and the environment in which we work influences and shapes our overall health and wellbeing. When we consider this from a collectivist perspective, we begin to understand *who* we share our environment with and *how* the spaces we occupy contribute to how happy, healthy, and comfortable we feel. We are all responsible for the part we play in contributing to the ecosystem's health and wellbeing in which we exist. Holistically speaking, we form a community, and to thrive, we cannot work only to think about ourselves individually. We must consider the whole community. Creating and cultivating an early years ecosystem where you belong takes time, effort, and patience. Too often, we try to fit in, squeeze, change and bend into spaces that are not the right fit for us. We can lose our way or forget our why, not know or fully realise our purpose, personal pedagogy, values, and beliefs. Many ecosystems face similar challenges and struggles. Many different risk factors get in the way and can disrupt our peace and have the potential to create wellbeing issues that affect the quality of provision and, in turn, the outcomes for children in our care. We can eliminate risk factors that act as barriers to staff health and harmony. Staff happiness is not a fluke. When we understand wellbeing as being at the heart of our ecosystem and focus on protective factors that nurture all of the community within it, this will enable us to flourish. In Figure i2.2 you can see how the core values I use in this book coexist and overlap, and weave together to create a mentally healthy workplace culture.

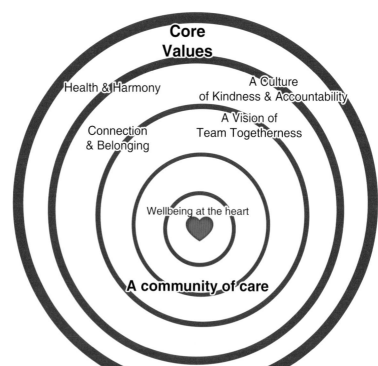

Figure i2.2 Core values within an early years ecosystem

Thinking about the EY ecosystem in which you work, reflect on the core values in Figure i2.2 to identify your own areas of strength and areas for development.

- Myself
- My team colleagues
- Children and families
- A community of care
- Team togetherness
- Connection and belonging
- Health and harmony
- A culture of kindness and accountability

Wellbeing issues

In Part 1, Chapter 1 discussed the concept of wellbeing issues within our EY ecosystems. Let us remind ourselves of what some common examples of wellbeing issues might be. Think about what causes you wellbeing issues at work? Use the blank template (see Figure i2.3) to reflect on your own?

(A copy of Figure 1.3 from Part 1 provided for reference)

Your Wellbeing Issues

Figure i2.3 Your wellbeing issues

This section will highlight how we can address these common and recurring situations that so many of us working in EY experience, that threaten our health, happiness, and job satisfaction. To do this, we will identify common factors that we determine as a risk to wellbeing and factors that can protect our wellbeing.

Risk and protective factors

Policies and procedures are legal and statutory requirements, but they are more than that. If effectual, they influence and guide everyday practice. It is not uncommon for EY settings to purchase templates and policies of all kinds rather than creating their own. This can be problematic if we do not consider the staff community they are for when writing them. Policies and procedures of any kind should be developed by and for the people who will implement them. So often, paperwork is written or viewed as a tick box exercise and then shoved away in a folder for regulatory purposes only. Folders containing pages and pages of policies and mission statements do not mean a thing if they have not been translated into everyday actions and practice. It is not just about testing or spot-checking staff if they know stuff ahead of inspections. It is how they are embodied and understood, and why that matters in the first place.

This is by no means an exhaustive list, but I have shown in Table 2.1 that by reviewing how effective and inclusive the settings systems and structures are, will indicate factors that can protect wellbeing, and ineffective systems and structures factors that put wellbeing at risk. No matter what role you work in, you can use the tables as the start of all the chapters in Part 2 of this book, as a reflective tool to consider your current role and the operation of the setting you in work in, to consider the impact this has on your wellbeing at work. However, if you work alone compared to a larger setting, for example, you will not have a commitment to employees, rather a commitment to yourself, your family and children, and families in your care. Overall, you can outline any aims or intentions that lead to any future actions you wish to put into place for long-term, sustainable improvements.

Table 2.1 Systems and structures

Wellbeing protective factors	Wellbeing risk factors

Inspiring and consistent leadership drives practice and cultivates a happy, healthy, and harmonious environment in which to work.
 	
There are clear and effective policies and procedures in place that meet and comply with statutory frameworks.
 	
There is clarity, fairness, and consistency around implementing policies and processes.
 	
The setting has developed its own policies and procedures, and all staff develop and evaluate them. Staff views are sought to understand, connect, and value cultural diversity, neurodivergence, gender identity, learning differences, physical disability, mental and physical health conditions.
 	
• Wellbeing
• Stress
• Mental health
• Sickness and absence
• Performance management
• New employees and induction
• Resilience
• Safeguarding
• Confidentiality
• Equality
• Inclusion
• Anti-racism
• Behaviour
• Lone working policy
• Staff handbook
   ○ Clear protocol for dealing with concerns/disclosures
   ○ Clear protocol for dealing with allegations against a member of staff, volunteer, manager, and proprietor
	Leadership is inadequate and ineffectual. Policies and procedures exist only to comply with statutory frameworks and:
	
	• do not inform and inspire practice
	• are not written, developed, reviewed, and evaluated by all staff
	• are not inclusive, no effort has been made to include staff perspectives of cultural beliefs and experiences, neurodivergence, gender identity, learning differences, physical disability, mental and physical health conditions
	• staff issues such as bullying, discrimination, racism, ageism, and sexism, ableism
	• policies involving parental guidance are tokenistic and there is ineffectual implementation, which leads to lots of niggles and complaints. This creates a lack of trust, such as complaints about a lack of communication, developmental progress, lack of clarity around learning, outdoor play, suitable clothing, complaints about staff practice/conduct, parent code of conduct, boundaries over arrival and leaving times, extra sessions, payments.

SPACE FOR REFLECTION

Which protective factors do you identify with?   Which risk factors do you identify with?

What evidence do I have for protective factors within my setting?

Case study reflection

Let us look at a hypothetical case study example that we can use to understand the risk and protective factors and how they support us to identify and address wellbeing issues.

UNNECESSARY JOBS

Beverly is a childminder and receives a compliance visit from Ofsted following a parent complaint. She has been operating for eight years and previously been graded as outstanding, and there had been no previous issues or compliance visits. Beverly employs two assistants, and they occupy a purpose-built building at the rear of the family home. There are a total of 23 children on the register, eight of which are before and after school club children and 15 children on the EYFS register. This Ofsted visit led to parents losing confidence in the quality of the learning opportunities and some parents were worried about their children's development and progress.

Very quickly Beverly put a few additional measures in place to reassure parents that the compliance visit was following procedure. This situation was extremely upsetting and worrying for the childminder and her assistants and they wanted to deal with this situation as best they could.

Unfortunately, because of their complaint, Beverly lost not only her confidence in her relationships with families but also her trust. She began to put even more additional measures in place to show how she had addressed this issue. This meant a lot of the daily procedures have been over complicated, and there is a lot of additional paperwork to complete. The assistants working with Beverly are spending increasing amounts of time on paperwork, which they do not have time for. They are concerned that Beverly has started doing lots of things to keep parents happy, but that actually means their attention and focus is taken away from the children. When Beverly suggests everyone has to start writing a weekly newsletter, which includes photos of the week, on top of the already new observations for each child, that has to be emailed to parents on new software, everyone feels unhappy. When one of the assistants tries to say something to Beverly, she says, "parents and children come first". When a child has an accident in the garden, Beverly is frantic; the assistant is so upset, frustrated, and unhappy about what is happening because this would not have happened if everyone was not so preoccupied with paperwork, observations, and tablets.

What are the risk factors in this case study?

Are there any risk factors in your own setting or role that get in the way of you doing your role?

What protective factors could help Beverly and her team of assistants?

FINAL THOUGHTS

Workplace wellness toolkit
See pages 89–90 for a reminder of some ideas to create your own.

Have you identified any actions in this section that need your attention?

References

Bronfenbrenner, U. (1979). *The Ecology of Human Development.* Cambridge, MA: Harvard University Press.

Cumming T. & Wong S. (2019). Towards a holistic conceptualisation of early childhood educators' work-related well-being. *Contemporary Issues in Early Childhood*, 20(3), 265–281. Available at: doi:10.1177/1463949118772573

MacBlain, S. (2018). Bronfenbrenner: children's learning in a wider context. Available at: www.parenta.com/2018/09/01/bronfen brenner-childrens-learning-in-a-wider-context/

4 | A vision of team togetherness

Exploring core values

This chapter is about the core value, team togetherness. A team connected and united by a shared vision of quality – an ethos that informs everyday practice, actions, expectations, and behaviours. Team togetherness interlinks with all other core values, especially connection and belonging, cultivating pride, and kinship. Think of it like your own EY family – all supporting and working alongside one another to accomplish your defined pedagogical ambition.

This core value will highlight the crucial role of early years managers and the quality of their leadership, which develops a sense of ambition that is underpinned by a clear vision and philosophy. Let me be clear, this is useful not only for leaders and managers themselves but for practitioners who wish to develop their own knowledge and expectations on leadership. This is crucially important to enable decision-making when we are applying for jobs or considering promotions.

If you are a small team or work alone, *you* are your team, and the families and children are an integral part of your togetherness. The same values and principles that this section develops are essential for lone workers, as a leader who aspires to the highest standards and has a clear philosophy that underpins everyday actions.

We will explore factors that protect our wellbeing and factors that put our wellbeing at risk. This is not an exhaustive list. There are many unique situations that you will experience in your role. However,

DOI: 10.4324/9781003146247-8

I have found that many common and recurring themes impact our health and happiness in the workplace, so I have given examples of what happens if the protective factors are not in place. Of course, some of the protective factors relate to statutory and legal guidance that strengthen everything from our systems and structures to daily actions.

When we embrace wellbeing in this way, we are moving away from just a narrow view of formal statutory and legal obligations. You are bringing core values to life in a way that shows you genuinely care about yourself and your colleagues as people, and when you invest in them, they invest in you, which is good for your business and has exceptional results for children. It makes sense then that happy employees create happy environments, which have good results for the business. Happiest Places to Work (2021) tells us, "Happiness is the most important human motivation", workplaces where staff report high levels of happiness are performing better, customer satisfaction is higher, there is less employee turnover, and there are higher levels of employee engagement.

WELLBEING MANIFESTO

Manifesto: our team declaration of intent

A manifesto is a declaration of our intentionality that clearly states the ethos that everyone follows; it is about your community of care. A manifesto is created and developed by all of your community; it is coming together to reflect on what is important to you, linked to core values that spell out your intentions for staff wellbeing.

A VISION OF TEAM TOGETHERNESS

Leadership is an integral part of a vision of team togetherness that cultivates pride and kinship. Inspirational leadership motivates and influences the community towards high standards and a shared vision of quality.

A WELLBEING MANIFESTO

Manifesto – a team declaration of intent
Our vision of wellbeing at the heart of all we do

The health and wellbeing of our EYE is a matter of importance to our whole community. Our educators are the key to the high-quality care that we pride ourselves on, and our unique ethos and approach are heart centric, developed around the needs of babies, children, and their families. We believe that if our staff are happy, healthy, and comfortable in their work environment, they are supported to flourish. They reach their full potential, enabling all our community to thrive.

The daily routine, operation, and organisation of our setting have been carefully cultivated to incorporate our philosophy of early childhood, the vision we hold with all children in mind, and this informs our everyday purpose, practice, and pedagogy. Our core values and beliefs shape the reciprocal relationship we develop with all our EYE.

Our wellbeing manifesto sets our clear leadership, management, and commitment to staff wellbeing that promotes our highly skilled educators' personal and professional development. We also believe that everyone within our community has a part to play in upholding our pedagogical values and beliefs that empower a personal and professional commitment to wellbeing.

The manifesto aims to represent our dedication to an integrated approach to staff wellbeing that is integrated into core values, that inspire our day-to-day practice and creates:

- A vision of team togetherness – underpinned by our clear vision and ethos
- A sense of connection and belonging – that cultivates trust, respect, and kinship
- Health and harmony – valuing resilience and protecting work-life balance
- A culture of kindness and accountability based on shared values and trust

Table 4.1 A vision of team togetherness

Protective factors	Risk factors
Inspirational leadership motivates staff and brings the vision of the setting and the core values to life.	Leadership is inconsistent and lacks vision. There is a lack of focus and drive.
• Leaders are organised and have a clear purpose, focus, and direction. Core values are observable through staff practice and in the quality of teaching and learning. • Staff and children exhibit high levels of wellbeing and self-esteem. • Leaders and staff model reflective practice that develops communication and aspirations of high-quality practice. • Leaders are aware of their areas of strength and areas for development.	• Leaders are apathetic. • Staff have no confidence in their leader. • There is a lack of trust in their leader; they are pulled in different directions and lack confidence in decision-making, causing conflict and disharmony. • Staff are unmotivated. • Staff are defensive and unable to model reflective practice. • There is little desire to identify areas of development to improve practice.
All staff work towards the same pedagogy, philosophy, vision, or ethos that underpins everything you do. It is clearly, concisely, and consistently communicated to all staff, parents, and all of the community.	There are no clear philosophy and pedagogical approach to inform practice.
• Yearly improvement plans focus on areas of development that ensure focussed and well-targeted training and professional development and are evaluated by all termly. • Partnerships with parents develop a shared understanding of a child-led ethos. Communication and information-sharing is a strength of the provision, and parents are clear on how their children learn and develop.	• Poor communication. • Unclear expectations. • Staff are unable to explain how children learn, grow, and develop in their care. • Practice is inconsistent; it does not inspire or motivate staff. • Staff morale is low. • There is no vision of what children can achieve. • The quality of the provision is affected as a result. • Parents have concerns about how their children are learning.
There is a staff handbook that exemplifies core values, staff practice, and professionalism.	There is no system in place that develops a professional working culture.
• High-quality standards develop a culture that elevates practice, and a community of care, based on dignity and respect. • This is evident and observable in the relationships and communication that staff have with each other, children and families.	• Staff overhear leaders share personal or sensitive information, and leaders do not model integrity towards confidentiality. • Leaders engage in gossip. • Leaders show favouritism. • Staff report issues with one another. • Staff morale is low. • There are no core values that support staff professionalism. • Expectations of staff are low. • Staff conflict is unresolved.

Protective factors	Risk factors
Training inspires staff, positively impacts practice, and improves outcomes for children. • Reflective practice drives the quality of the provision. Staff display self-awareness and are able to make accurate judgements linked to areas of strength and areas for development.	Training is inconsistent and not targeted. It is ineffectual and does not drive improvement. • Training is organised ad hoc and last minute. • Staff do not attend training. • Staff are not paid to attend training. • Staff do not understand the rationale for the training.
• Staff have a love for ongoing personal development. • Staff have the opportunity to attend training and engage in continuous professional and personal development. • Through performance management, staff can identify and attend training and professional development opportunities.	• Staff views are not considered, which affects career development and progression. • Training only relates to the impact of children • Staff and leaders do not utilise opportunities for informal professional development; for example, podcasts, magazines, reading, webinars.

SPACE FOR REFLECTION

Which protective factors do you identify with?   Which risk factors do you identify with?

What evidence do I have for protective factors within my setting?

Leadership

Would you be interested in learning factors that impact on staff turnover linked to poor company leadership and a negative company culture, rather than salary or workload stress? There is a big difference between managing people and leading people. Leading people requires influence, and the ability to inspire others, cultivating reciprocal relationships to accomplish something, leading others towards achievement.

Is the leadership in your setting guiding your community towards your shared vision or philosophy? So often, I speak with managers who have got stuck managing the setting they are responsible for rather than *leading* the people working within the setting. Sadly, I see managers who have no time for their people because they are doing all of the things, and sometimes lots of unnecessary things, for other people. I know this because I have been there too. I have made many mistakes and questionable decisions along the way. As I have told you earlier in the book, I was leading and managing people for many, many years without having ever had any formal leadership training. I was learning from the people who led and managed me! When you work with children, you come into the role because you enjoy working with children, or maybe most of us do! We do not think about leading and managing people at the start. Still, if you are skilled in your role, then your position may progress to increasing responsibility, such as leading and managing others as your career develops. Leading and managing people is overwhelming, especially so in EY, due to the sheer amount of responsibility. That is why this whole book is based upon personal and professional development. It will take a shift in mindset, how you think and feel about yourself, and how you inspire and lead others towards a vision of team togetherness.

What is a leader?

"Anyone who takes responsibility for finding the potential in people and processes and has the courage to develop that potential".
Brené Brown has spent over twenty years studying courage, vulnerability, shame, and empathy, and a seven-year study on brave leadership. *Dare to Lead* (2018) is about taking off the armour that we use to protect ourselves and show up as all of who we are as aspiring leaders. Suggestions that came from the brave leadership study on leadership skills are:

- You can't get to courage without rumbling with vulnerability. Embrace the suck.
- Self-awareness and self-love matter. Who we are is how we lead.
- Courage is contagious.

(Brown, 2021)

Developing your pedagogical vision

RACHEL'S CASE STUDY
A philosophy of wellbeing

At the beginning of my journey, I am not ashamed to say I had a remarkably simple vision – to get children outside into nature. Beyond that, I was not sure. Some say this was foolish, and for a time, I was inclined to concur; but as the months rolled by, I began to see the benefits of developing a vision with not only my team but the children and families too. I can only describe (as I often do to new families) that in those early days, we simply walked alongside the children and by doing so, we learnt so much about ourselves and them. We slowly began to think about our professional and personal values and why these were so important and intrinsic to practice. We spent many months talking about what would be our "why" and how we would share this with others (including Ofsted). It felt as though we had begun to shape practice based on our aligned views as a team, and this meant that we were then able to develop a shared rationale that truly reflected our vision – putting children at the heart of everything.

We wanted everyone to recognise this, so we began to think about how our behaviours would demonstrate this to new families, new staff, and other stakeholders. How would they know that we had a truly child-led and enabling environment? How could we convey the nurture we were keen to offer? The small staff team at the time worked together; we shared our thoughts and feelings, our whys and wants. A very clear vision and pedagogical approach was born. Practitioners owned it; families believed in it because we were able to talk about it in a way that was accessible for all. Even the children bear the hallmarks of what we now call a children's rights-based model in which voices and choices are respected.

When new staff join us, we want them to feel the same sense of agency as our children and their families. We want them to feel it, understand it, and make sure that their views about childhood echo ours. It's non-negotiable; practitioners need to feel it and come to work at Beatle Woods (BW) because they believe in our vision and approach completely. With this comes high levels of wellbeing and self-esteem for our teams. They shape practice themselves. We have recently grown our team significantly, and with this comes the worry about all of the above. However, we empower our staff as we do the children. It is vital that they have ownership about what day-to-day practice looks like and because we have a clear vision and pedagogical approach, this is not only possible but a reality.

Rachel Macbeth-Webb is the owner and founder of the Beatle Woods Outdoor Nursery. Nursery World Winner of the Enabling Environment Award. https://beatlewoods.co.uk/

Case study

Let us look at a hypothetical case study example that we can use to apply the risk and protective factors to identify and address wellbeing issues.

 WELLBEING BASKETS

Paula has recently been promoted to nursery manager in a small PVI setting. She loves working with children but is trying to get to grips with her new responsibilities as a manager. She feels that staff are demotivated and have shown little interest in her attempts for team building ideas, staff meetings or training. She has started avoiding spending time in the rooms with staff and children, as she finds some of the long-standing staff members difficult. She quite enjoys the admin, and there is so much paperwork to organise and get on top of. Paula decides to create a staff wellbeing basket for the team and a staff shout-out board, because it has been a busy and stressful time lately. Paula gives a lot of care and attention to selecting the items for it, and it takes up most of her working week and weekend. She ends up spending much more time and money than she anticipated. She gets into work even earlier than usual on Monday and sets it up in the staff room. When she pops back in after lunch, she discovers it is virtually empty; staff did say thank you, but nobody has really mentioned it and how much time and effort it must have taken her. Paula feels a little hurt that everyone has helped themselves and not really been grateful. Paula will not say anything to the team because she does not like confrontation and finds it uncomfortable to discuss things that others might not want to hear. She tells her deputy manager Sam how she feels, knowing she will probably make it known for her and ends up avoiding the staff room and the staff for the rest of the week. Paula notices a few of the staff have responded to the shout-out board, but not everyone has joined in. She wonders why she bothers; she does not have the time or the energy to follow through with the shout-out board; she thinks there is no point as nobody will pay attention anyway. Sam tells the staff in her room that Paula is not very happy, and before long, all the staff are talking about it. They feel frustrated and cross because although it was nice to have the surprise in the staff room and Paula is brilliant with children and parents, when it comes to staffing issues, nothing tends to get followed through, and they have learnt not to bother. All staff really want is the opportunity to have the performance management 1:1 discussion as promised.

- What are your immediate thoughts?
- How would you feel if you were Paula?
- What would it be like to work here?
- How would this affect practice?
- What are the risk factors here?
- How can the protective factors begin to address these issues?

Leaders and managers that cultivate a community

What is it like to be a member of staff here? What contributes to the health, happiness, and job satisfaction of your community?

Think again here about the early years educator that you are today, building or reflecting from the earlier chapter, think about why you work where you do today. So often, the wellbeing issues affecting us are because we are trying to fit in somewhere that we do not belong. Why have you chosen to share your unique skills, strengths, talents, qualifications, career-long professional development with the organisation or family you are employed in, or the self-employed business you own and run today? As a leader how do you empower members of your community?

REFLECTION QUESTIONS

1. I feel valued as a part of the setting's community.
2. I am proud when I tell others I am part of this setting.
3. I would recommend this school as a great place to work.
4. I feel a strong personal attachment to this setting.
5. This setting inspires me to do the best in my job.
6. This setting motivates me to help it achieve its objectives.
7. I enjoy my job role and feel fulfilled and accomplished.
8. I have an acceptable workload.
9. I have been given the training and support I need to complete my job role to the best of my ability.
10. I have had the opportunity to access professional development opportunities organised and provided by line managers/head-teacher within my usual working hours in the past 12 months, which has helped improve my performance.
11. I have completed professional development opportunities in my own time over the past 12 months, which has helped improve my performance.
12. There are opportunities for me to develop my career in this setting.
13. My manager has recognised my skills and strengths, and I am encouraged to learn and share practice with my colleagues.
14. My manager has made efforts to learn, understand, and get to know my cultural and religious background, views, and beliefs.
15. I am my whole self at work and share the intersections of my identity.
16. My setting is culturally competent and understands the concept of deep culture.
17. I am happy with the way performance management is organised and find supervisions and appraisals are effective and worthwhile.
18. My line manager motivates me to be more effective in my job.
19. My line manager is open to my ideas.
20. I think that my performance is evaluated fairly
21. Issues that arise are dealt with sensitively and effectively.
22. If I am worried or upset about something that has happened at work, I feel comfortable talking to my line manager about it.
23. I am happy with how changes are communicated to me and have a say in the most significant changes.

24. When changes are made, I am clear on how they will work out in practice.
25. I am actively involved in the setting's self-evaluation and have the opportunity to identify areas of priority for improvement.
26. The setting's values, vision, and mission statement, underpin my role and daily responsibilities.
27. As a team, we can rely upon each other to help when things get difficult.
28. As a team, we can rely upon each other and find ways to improve our provision.
29. Does this school respect individual differences (e.g. cultures, working styles, backgrounds, ideas, etc.)?
30. All staff treat all children fairly and with respect.
31. Staff work well to understand and support children's behaviour.
32. All staff treat each other fairly and with respect.
33. Staff and parents usually treat each other fairly and with respect.
34. Staff communicate effectively with each other.
35. I achieve a good balance between my work life and private life.
36. The staff room is a suitable space and environment to enjoy my lunch and have a restful break.
37. I am given sufficient notice of staff meetings or training that I am expected to attend after work.
38. If you could change one thing about your role, what would it be?
39. What do you enjoy the least about your role and responsibilities?
40. What do you enjoy the most about your role and responsibilities?
41. How happy have you felt at work this week?
42. If you could be the manager for the day, what would you do differently?
43. When you think of the working week ahead on Sunday evening, how do you feel?
44. What training would I like to complete?
45. Where do I see myself in the future? The next five years?

Further questions for nannies or childminders

1. Are you registered with a childminding or nanny agency?
2. Are you part of your local professional support groups? Or have you developed professional relationships with other childminders/nannies locally?

3. If I am worried or upset about something that has happened at work, I feel comfortable that I can talk to my families.
4. If I am having difficulty or issues with parents, I can follow policies and procedures and avoid conflict.
5. I seek parents' views regularly, which promotes our professional relationship and enables me to evaluate my provision and make necessary improvements.
6. Childminders/nannies and parents treat each other fairly and with respect.
7. I find parents demanding and difficult?
8. I have an acceptable workload.
9. Childminders, do you actively complete a self-evaluation of the setting and identify areas of priority for improvement?
10. The setting's values, vision and mission statement, underpin my role and daily responsibilities.
11. Childminders, how do you manage to find a balance with your family/home life whilst running a business from home? For example, do you model good working practices and self-care to encourage an appropriate work-life balance?
12. I schedule times for rest or breaks/lunch where possible.

Achieving that vision

How will you know your protective factors are creating a vision for team togetherness?

You will see how the core values promote the protective factors and bring them to life. They will be visible in the everyday actions of the whole community. There is an openness for improvement and collaboration.

As a team and/or in collaboration with families, discuss what a vision of team togetherness would look, feel and sound like in everyday practice. What would be the impact on staff, children, families and the quality of the overall provision?

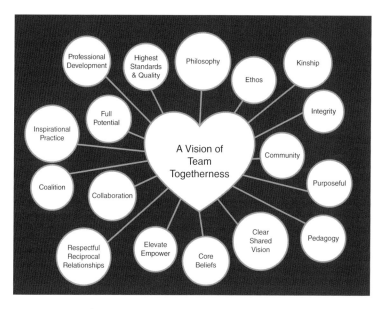

Figure 4.1 A vision of team togetherness

 **FINAL THOUGHTS**

Workplace wellness toolkit
See pages 89–90 for a reminder of some ideas to create your own.

Have you identified any actions in the 'Core value: a vision of team togetherness' section that need your attention?

References

Brown, Brené. (2018). *Dare to Lead:* Brave Work. Tough Conversations. Whole Hearts. Vermilion.

Brown, Brené. (2021). Power of Vulnerability. TED talk.

Happiest Places to Work. (2021). Available at: www.happiestplacesto work.org/blog/2021/3/10/happiness-at-work-is-so-important-that-it-can-predict-whether-a-company-will-survive-or-not

5 | Connection and belonging

Exploring core values

Connection and belonging are essential for any EY community, not just between educators and children but also with colleagues and a whole team, to enable professional attachments that will allow us to identify our individual and collective skills, strengths, and talents.

We all have an intrinsic need to connect with others and feel a sense of belonging. As caregivers, a considerable part of our role is cultivating connection and belonging with babies, children, and families in our care. We do this in all sorts of everyday ways without even thinking about it.

When we genuinely accomplish a sense of belonging, it enables us to feel valued, improves staff health, motivation, and happiness. A philosophy based on connectedness and belongingness promotes a community culture of trust, respect, and dignity. It raises professionalism and the quality of our everyday practice and provision.

The lived experience case studies in this chapter will enable the reader to contemplate scenarios that highlight areas of development and examples of areas of strength. The reflection questions will encourage us to consider strategies that can develop a connection and belonging within our roles; be it individual relationships, smaller teams that work together, or larger staff teams. Whatever your job role you can use the risk and protective factors to reflect on your own professional practice and the environment in which you work.

DOI: 10.4324/9781003146247-9

CONNECTION AND BELONGING

Connection is a feeling, an ease and understanding in a relationship where people feel seen, heard, valued, and accepted.

Belongingness is our place within our community and an affinity for that place.

 Table 5.1 Connection and belonging

Protective factors	Risk factors
Inclusive leadership ensures an intersectional approach to wellbeing so that all members of the community are treated respectfully and fairly. • Staff feel valued and have the sense that they belong, feel confident, and inspired. • Leadership drives an authentic commitment to diversity. • Leaders are culturally intelligent – there is a deep concept of culture and respect for different cultures. • Systems and structures are disability and gender-inclusive. • Staff feel comfortable and connected to each other.	Leadership lacks inclusivity. • Leadership lacks cultural competency and leaders do not learn about cultural differences. • Understanding of culture is surface-level only. • Staff do not take the time to learn or understand each other's cultures. • Staff access needs are not met. • Staff feel isolated at work.
The philosophy for learning and the ethos and values of the setting are woven throughout all aspects of the recruitment process, and led and supported by emotionally intelligent managers and practice. • Efforts are made to ensure prospective early years educators are aligned with the philosophy of the setting, from job adverts, interviews, show arounds and open days. • Adjustments have been considered to ensure diversity in the recruitment process that creates intentionality around hiring staff from different backgrounds, such as race, ethnicity, sexuality, gender, physical and mental health conditions. This is considered through job advertisement and application.	Little thought or consideration is given to recruitment and how it can be effectively organised to ensure candidates share and understand the philosophy of the setting right from the start. • Expectations are not formally shared through recruitment, job appointment or induction. • Prospective candidates do not state valuable information on application forms as they do not feel safe disclosing parts of their identity and hide parts of their identity. • The setting and children that attend it do not benefit from a diverse workforce, and there is a lack of representation in the form of ethnicity, gender, disability. • Staff turnover is high.

Protective factors	Risk factors
• Through a focused and targeted induction programme, there is a clear system of support that ensures all new starting educators have received everything they need to fulfil their job role and responsibilities. • There is an induction handbook for new employees. • Job advertisements and job offers outline clear information-sharing around salary, working hours, overtime, holidays, wages, and organisational benefits, i.e. Employee Assistance Programme (EAP).	• Staff recruitment and retention is an ongoing issue. • Unqualified and inexperienced or new staff are working with children without support or guidance.
Timelines are organised each academic year effectively, with supervision, 1:1 appraisals, room meetings, staff meetings, inset training days, team building days and so that these are mutually beneficial and reciprocal processes that drive improvement through the continuing personal and professional development of all educators.	There is little or no organisation for performance management. • Performance management does not drive improvement. • Staff report wellbeing issues. • They are not dealt with in a timely manner. • Staff are complacent. • Staff sickness and absence is an issue. • Ratios are not consistently met. • The quality of provision is affected. • Policies and procedures are not followed.
Performance management is well-organised and worthwhile, drives improvement, promotes connection and belonging, and is a reciprocal process between the line manager and staff member. • Staff's protected characteristics inform provision, and reasonable adjustments are made as necessary as per the Equality Act, 2010. • Paperwork linked to staff performance is reviewed annually or on a rolling programme, and all staff are encouraged to contribute and evaluate. • All staff understand and know what is expected of them and have had all the relevant training and support needed to fulfil their job description. • Performance management develops open and honest communication that encourages staff participation, so that all staff feel safe and secure to share their thoughts, feelings, and ideas.	There is little or no formal induction programme in place. Staff do not receive a job description with a complete outline of roles and responsibilities. • Managers have completed little or no leadership training, such as on performance management. • Leaders fail to follow through with agreed actions. • Leaders treat staff as an inconvenience. • Staff have little say or motivation in professional development and little aspiration for career progression. • Staff with named responsibilities, such as SENCO, Wellbeing Champion, DSL are not given recognition or capacity to complete the role.

Protective factors	Risk factors
• Self-esteem is high as staff are proud of their achievements, know their skills, strengths, and talents and share them with colleagues. • Staff are well-supported to develop a reflective practice that supports healthy methods that identify areas for development. • Staff with named roles are equipped to carry out their responsibilities.	

SPACE FOR REFLECTION

Which protective factors do you identify with?

Which risk factors do you identify with?

What evidence do I have for protective factors within my setting?

A community of care

Rethinking how we heal and support one another

As much as we have a personal responsibility to take care of ourselves, we also deserve the professional responsibility from the organisations in which we choose to work. Carol Garboden Murray (2020) calls this a "community of care" and states, "if we work in institutions and systems that neglect to operate with care as a core value, and refuse basic rights of care workers, we are all doomed to abuse ourselves, mistreat one another, and diminish care itself". This leads us to consider how our wellbeing is so much more than self-care, and collectively combine our personal and professional identities to understand our wellbeing.

Nakita Valerio, a Muslim woman, living in New Zealand, went viral with her Facebook status, *"Shouting 'self-care' at people who actually need community care is how we fail people".*

This was the result of the trauma and grief at the terrorist attack in Christchurch, where 50 Muslim worshippers lost their lives. Interestingly, Valerio shares her perspective on being a millennial – burnt out from a generation told we can have and be it all and dealing with ongoing trauma and oppression. The reaction from the viral post led to an overwhelming response from other marginalised communities, from racial and religious minorities, disability advocates, LGBTQIA+ persons, all of whom were enduring similar experiences affecting their mental health, but merely being told self-care is the answer.

Self-care is not enough. We need community care to thrive.

"Self-care is about the individual caring for their own basic physical needs, whereas community care is focused on the collective: taking care of people together, for everything from basic physical needs to psychological and even spiritual ones. Community care is a recognition of the undeniable cooperative and social nature of human beings and involves a commitment to reduce harm simply through being together".

Nakita Valerio

150

When we are able to embed a philosophy of wellbeing at the heart of our practice, shaped and formed into core values and beliefs, it can create a community of care, so we leave behind one-off gestures that are ill-thought-out and feel like a token gesture, that leave us feeling uneasy, unhappy with one another and misunderstood. The answer is not self-care. It is a workplace where we all look out for each other. Workplaces that are investing in their people, through employee assistance programmes (EAPs), with free access to psychological therapies, such as counselling, cognitive behavioural therapies, online training and support, human resources, occupational health, with a menu of supportive methods that enable people to thrive and stay in work, through various performance management supports, wellness action plans, workplace pressure support plans, reasonable adjustments, trained mental health first aiders and mental health champions, all cultivate a mental health workplace community, based on open, honest and transparent communication. As Valerio describes it, community care means: "People committed to leveraging their privilege to be there for one another in various ways".

Supporting our LGBTQIA+ colleagues and celebrating diversity

FIFI'S STORY

"Feeling connected to colleagues is an important protective factor in reducing workplace stress".

Having experienced different settings, different managers, and gradually changing staff teams, I appreciate how feeling valued and trusted by my team has improved my mental health and made me better at my job. Being a young adult with no children, I found it easy to feel underqualified and doubt my instincts at work. Building better relationships with colleagues really changed that for me. Being part of a team that works together to solve problems, and having colleagues who ask for my opinion or reassurance, has helped minimise my insecurities about not being good enough. I am still the youngest in my staff team but I feel respected as a special educational needs and disabilities coordinator (SENDCo) and deputy manager by colleagues who understand that age, experience, and ability are all separate factors that don't follow a single set path.

It is especially important to me as a disabled person to create spaces where people can be open when something is difficult or impossible for them. A part of this happens in supervisions and a part is much less formal. It can be extremely difficult to admit when something is wrong at work, but nothing will change if it cannot be addressed. The only way to make this easier is to build trust through consistent communication. Staff need to know that expressing distress isn't going to result in disciplinary action or be resented. We all have our own needs in terms of accessibility, shifts, workload, development etc. and we should be able to have those needs met wherever possible by management. Staff teams should feel able to have honest conversations about how they are.

Something I hope changes in our sector is the lack of diversity amongst professionals. Being queer is an important part of my identity and the community I've found through that is where I feel safest. This can then make it more difficult to connect with colleagues when I know none of them share that community with me. I know that members of other minoritised communities feel the same in our sector, more so people of colour as tokenism and ignoring oppression are huge problems in our sector. I hope that the recent surge in seeking out anti-racism and anti-oppression training results in material changes that allow our sector to become a safer space for people from minoritised communities.

Fifi Benham is a pre-school deputy manager, SENDCo and writer. https://earlyyearsactivism.wordpress.com/home/

A culturally responsive community

The iceberg concept of culture (Hall, 1976) can be used in EY practice to illuminate culture and cultural differences and we can use this to consider contrasting attitudes to wellbeing. It shows us what may be visible or *invisible*

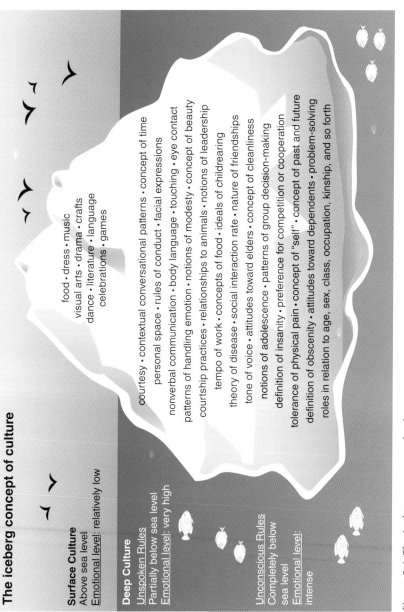

The iceberg concept of culture

Surface Culture
Above sea level
Emotional level: relatively low

food · dress · music
visual arts · drama · crafts
dance · literature · language
celebrations · games

Deep Culture
Unspoken Rules
Partially below sea level
Emotional level: very high

courtesy · contextual conversational patterns · concept of time
personal space · rules of conduct · facial expressions
nonverbal communication · body language · touching · eye contact
patterns of handling emotion · notions of modesty · concept of beauty
courtship practices · relationships to animals · notions of leadership
tempo of work · concepts of food · ideals of childrearing
theory of disease · social interaction rate · nature of friendships
tone of voice · attitudes toward elders · concept of cleanliness
notions of adolescence · patterns of group decision-making
definition of insanity · preference for competition or cooperation
tolerance of physical pain · concept of "self" · concept of past and future
definition of obscenity · attitudes toward dependents · problem-solving
roles in relation to age, sex, class, occupation, kinship, and so forth

Unconscious Rules
Completely below
sea level
Emotional level:
intense

Figure 5.1 The iceberg concept of culture

153

to us if we only see culture at the surface level. Suppose we only view what is visible on the surface level, like food, dress, music, arts, crafts, dance, literature, language, festivals, and celebrations. In that case, we may see an incomplete perspective of a person's identity and culture. This may make our relationships surface level and lack authenticity, leading to a lack of trust, connection, or belonging. Before we can understand the cultural norms of another, we must first understand *our own* frame of reference and cultural norms. This must lead us to consider the colleagues we work alongside and how we acknowledge our individual racial, cultural, and ethnic identities on an authentic cultural level to avoid tokenism and address incidents of racism (Tembo, 2020).

Thinking about the iceberg concept of culture, revisit the risk and protective factors at the start of the chapter to reflect on how inclusive your community is.

Is your community surface level or embedding a deeper understanding of culture for all of your community – staff, children, and families?

Anti-racist EY practice

In EY we tend to think of racism as an overt action or behaviour rather than considering the systems and structures that we conform to in the daily operational practice of the setting and the statutory policy and guidance that we follow. It is not enough to say you aren't racist, you have to be anti-racist. Read the following definitions from Ibram X. Kendi (2020).

Racist: one who is supporting a racist policy through their actions or inaction or expressing a racist idea.

Anti-racist: one who is supporting an anti-racist policy through their actions or expressing an antiracist idea.

Liz Pemberton, the Black Nursery Manager, tells us that "racism is a conscious act" and that "conflating acts of racism with a state of unconsciousness suggests that the perpetrator is not aware of how to treat other people with a basic level of humanity". Anti-racism practice is fundamentally about basic human rights and, as Liz says, "is a focus on how we dismantle the structures that uphold racism in the early years sector".

LIZ PEMBERTON, THE BLACK NURSERY MANAGER

My 4 E's of anti-racist practice are a framework for practitioners to use to help them to implement anti-racist strategies whilst engaging with children, but it is also a framework that I think can be adapted to be applied to the way in which practitioners interact with one another within their setting too.

Working towards creating an environment where people feel as though they belong as opposed to feeling as though they are included into an already established way of doing things (which is entrenched within the dominant culture of white supremacist patriarchal "norms") are two very different things. As a Black woman who has worked in the early years for 17 years in various capacities – a practitioner, a nursery manager, a teacher of childcare, and a trainer and consultant, the lens through which I have been able to see and feel belonging is directly impacted because of the way in which my identity markers intersect.

I am acutely aware that although I have been involved in the sector in a variety of roles, I am still very often the only Black person in spaces that proclaim to be "inclusive". This is not just anecdotal but statistically supported by data that Shaddai Tembo draws upon in his 2020 journal paper, Black educators in (white) settings: Making racial identity visible in Early Childhood Education and Care in England, UK. His paper is an important and necessary read.

Liz Pemberton, The Black Nursery Manager, is a trainer and consultant specialising in anti-racism in early years and education. www.theblacknurserymanager.com/

Figure 5.2 TBNM 4E's for anti-racist practice

Creating connection and belonging

What is like to be a new member of staff here?

Think about starting in a new provision, how do you support staff from interview, through to job offer, induction, probationary period, and beyond. How do they get the best support from you so that you get the best quality practice from them?

ONBOARDING AT HOPES & DREAMS BY LAURA PEIRCE

What is onboarding?

We have a 90-day staff retention plan that is shared with all of our managers.

"When new staff are just thrown into a room, they can also feel neglected, like they were not important enough to be given proper training. They will feel uncertain about what is expected of them, make assumptions and be worried that they are doing something wrong or making the wrong choice. They can be overwhelmed when they don't start out on the right foot, and quickly question their decision to take a job at your nursery". Sindye Alexander (Relationship Roadmap)

As soon as all the pre-employment checks are completed and before their first day at nursery, the new recruit receives a handwritten "Welcome" card from Gary and I as owners, a "Welcome" card from their new manager and they are also introduced on our internal staff Facebook group with some information about them, and maybe a fun fact.

The Friday before the new recruit is due to start work, their manager sends them an email letting them know what to expect on their first day; for example, where to park, what to bring and a brief explanation about what will happen in their first two days in work. This hopefully answers those questions that can get forgotten or can weigh on people's minds thinking, is that a daft question to ask!

We have lots of things ready for Day One, just like we do for when new children start. Some of these things include a "Welcome" card from all staff at their new setting, a labelled locker, a welcome on our public Facebook page, a new day starter kit (Hopes & Dreams mug with their name on, a hand sanitiser and pen that can clip onto a lanyard, a key ring, chocolate bar, and some tissues).

We encourage the managers to chat with the new member of staff before they head home at the end of their first day or give them a call that night to see how their first day has gone.

The first two days are the start of the 90-day induction process. The morning of their first day is spent with the manager going through our core values, explaining "Family Share", which is our online learning portal for staff and parents, reminding them of the staff handbook, and then there is induction around our key procedures, such as fire and first aid.

On Family Share we have set up a first-day quiz, which involves the staff member reading key policies and procedures and then answering an online quiz around these. The rest of the day is then spent observing in the childcare room.

Day Two for the new recruit starts with observing in the childcare room in the morning and then in the afternoon they complete a scavenger hunt looking for all those things you may never get told where they are; for example, where the supply of paper towels are kept, where are the top-up nappy supplies kept, and where are the holiday request forms!

At the end of the first week and second week, I send an email to the new recruit to check how their first and second week has been. I check in with them as to whether they had all the information to hand when they started and whether their induction is going okay as well. I also pass on comments that their manager may have made about them settling into the team.

On the Saturday at the end of their first week they receive a gift in the post sent to their house from Gary and I as a thank you for joining the Hopes & Dreams family.

Throughout the year, all members of staff receive on their birthday a handwritten card and a gift in the post from Gary and I and on their first anniversary of being in the Hopes & Dreams family I write them a card and so does the manager.

After 90 days of working in Hopes & Dreams each member of staff has their 90-day review with their manager based on our core values, their knowledge of our policies and procedures and interactions with our families. At this point the member of staff sets their goals for the next six to nine months and they will have completed their probationary period with us. If the staff member and manager feels that the probationary period needs to be extended it will be.

Once a member of staff has been with us for six months the manager will ask if the member of staff will do a testimonial for us about their employment so far. These testimonials get put on our website and are used when we recruit.

To sum up, it's really important to both Gary and I that staff feel welcomed into the Hopes & Dreams family and that they know who we are. This breaks down any barriers when we go into settings, we know all the people that we employ. From Day One I am part of the recruitment process. An initial enquiry comes in about working for Hopes & Dreams and I give the person a call to find out more about them and to tell them more about us. If at the time we don't have any vacancies, then I ask if they would be happy to stay on our database and if a vacancy comes up that I feel they would be a good fit for them I get back in touch with them.

Hiring on attitude rather than just knowledge and skills is really important to us. Our Core Values are an important part of our recruitment and onboarding process.

It's so important to make the onboarding of staff successful. It's hard starting a new job, learning new routines, getting to know new adults and children, so taking away some anxiety from this process by having a clear procedure in place to make new staff feel welcomed and included is really important for the wellbeing of all.

"Even if the staff member is super experienced don't just throw them into the room. We don't know how they were trained previously. They don't know OUR policies and procedures. They need to spend some time in training becoming acquainted with our way of serving our clients and families. Ideally, new hires should not be counted in the ratio for at least a week. They don't know which blanket belongs to Jamie, where to get paper towel refills or which children have allergies so it can be overwhelming for both the seasoned practitioner and the newbie for different reasons. It's not safe for the children in our care if the newbie is still becoming acclimated to the building and surroundings. We don't want them to feel frustrated or overwhelmed in their first few days on the job. They will question whether they are adequate for the role and whether or not they should stick it out or not. If we follow the 90-day plan then current staff won't feel overworked and annoyed by having to work with people who don't know what they are doing and new staff will feel supported and more confident in their new positions". Sindye Alexander (Relationship Roadmap)

REFLECTION SPACE

Thoughts to consider

What is your onboarding process?
Think about the last time you started a new job, how did it feel? What worked well?
What didn't work so well? What could you change for the future?
What are the risk factors that you can recognise? What were the protective factors?

ROCHELLE ROBB, FOUNDING DIRECTOR, I AM? ME!©

I am an EYFS Lead – working in a borough of high deprivation.
I am from African Caribbean heritage.
Dyslexic.
Single mother of two children who live the life of having a Teacher Mum.

Always making sure I am in the room to speak for myself and others alike. I work extra hard to dispel any stereotypes that come with the many categories I might fall within.

My passion for the early years drives my decisions in life and helped found my business, I am? ME!© with other like-minded women. I am? ME!© is an early years CIC that creates resources and advice around the representation of African Caribbean heritage within the early years.

Creating connections and belongingness happens at all stages of the job process from advertisement, training, day-to-day and exit interviews. All these aspects allow for a healthy work life and promote good well-being.

Is this the right job for me?

- Advertise your setting and its ethos and its unique demographics and the positive challenges that inspire you to do what you do. Rather than just the job. The connections starts from the beginning by showcasing its USPs (unique selling points).
- I often work in Faith schools that have values that serve the community and encourage community.
- I enjoy working in deprived inner city early years settings with a range of barriers to learning. I will be inspired by these factors and will feel motivated to be employed to make a change.
- Let's market the job at the rate it deserves. You get what you pay for. It allows for consistency in commitment. Employees want to know they are getting paid for what they are doing. Not that money is everything, but you will feel happy if the pay equates to the responsibilities of the role.
- In early years our roles are multi-faceted and appreciation through pay gives an acknowledgment of the dedication that will be given.
- Be open and transparent and no illusions
- Encourage visits, allow for stay and plays. You want those who want be here because they share your vision rather than those that just want a job. The latter is not bad but where I have interacted with as many people during the recruitment stage I have had connections before even going into the job on my first day and from there they get stronger.

Being able to be at a leadership level is a privilege. I take pride in being of African Caribbean heritage and ensure my experiences are used to support my staff, children, and their parents. I love that I am able to challenge and make change. From a culture that sees mental health as a taboo, it's been an active role in my every day and I know now more than ever it requires managing like everything else in my life.

Case study reflection

Let us look at a hypothetical case study example that we can use to apply the risk and protective factors to identify and address wellbeing issues.

SUPPORTING NEW STAFF

Jamie is a cisgender man who recently qualified as an early years educator and who has started working in a nursery; he works with a small team of 16 people, including two room leaders, a deputy, and a manager. The deputy is responsible for induction and completing performance management. Jamie is enjoying the job role but finding one of the room leaders quite tricky. They are short-tempered every time he tries to ask questions about planning or setting up, and he is still trying to get the hang of using the iPad for observations and learn the way everything works. Jamie has been finding induction support valuable, as he feels comfortable asking questions, especially about the things he feels unable to ask his room leader. When the deputy has an accident and is suddenly signed off work, Jamie asks his manager who will support his induction, and he is told not to worry, and they will sort it soon. Nobody mentions it again, and Jamie is starting to feel worried about coming into work. Then a parent comments on Jamie doing nappies and toileting. This has never happened to him before, but he has heard friends at college talk about it when covering a module on gender. He feels like his room leader is talking about him behind his back, and he starts being put on outdoor duty a lot and realises he is no longer assisting with the toileting/nappy rota. He does not know who to talk to. Jamie has received no further feedback on how he is settling in, he has not received the next stage of induction support, and it is starting to affect his confidence and motivation and he is thinking of handing in his notice.

- What would you do immediately to support Jamie?
- What are the risk factors here?
- Which protective factors, had they been in place, could have helped support Jamie?

A culture of connection and belonging

How will you know your protective factors are cultivating connection and belonging?
You will see how the core values promote the protective factors and bring them to life. They will be visible in the everyday actions of the whole community. There is an openness for improvement and collaboration.

As a team, and/or in collaboration with families, discuss what true inclusion, and belonging would look, feel, and sound like in everyday practice? What would this require from leaders and staff? What would the impact be on staff, children, families, and the quality of the overall provision? Choose your own unique setting, specific behaviours or characteristics. I have given some examples in Figure 5.3.

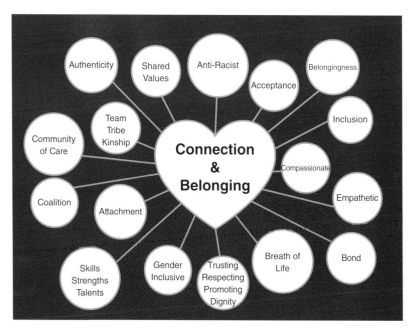

Figure 5.3 Connection and belonging

FINAL THOUGHTS

Workplace wellness toolkit
See pages 89–90 for a reminder of some ideas to create your own.

Have you identified any actions in the 'Core value: connection and belonging' section that need your attention?

References

Alexander, S. (2018). Relationship Roadmap: Real-World Strategies for Building a Positive, Collaborative Culture in Your Preschool.

Hall, Edward T. (1976). *Beyond Culture*. Garden City, NY: Anchor Press.

Kendi, Ibram X. (2020). *How to Be an Antiracist*. London: Penguin.

Murray, C.G. (2020). Available at: https://www.carolgarbodenmurray.com/blog/self-care-and-community-care-how-do-we-care-how-do-we-fail

Tembo, Shaddai. (2020). Black educators in (white) settings: Making racial identity visible in Early Childhood Education and Care in England. *Journal of Early Childhood Research*. Available at: doi: 10.1177/1476718X20948927

Health and harmony

Exploring core values

This core value sets out our clear intentionality on health and wellbeing. We cannot take risks with our health, and we must place a great emphasis on taking care of ourselves and each other. Unfortunately, we know issues in our roles and environment that, if they are not quickly addressed, however small, have the potential to affect how happy, healthy, and comfortable we feel at work.

In the other chapters, we have addressed the risk factors that act as barriers to our job satisfaction. The more protective factors we have in place the more we are enabled to have firm systems and structures that promote health and harmony for all of us, children, and families. This chapter builds on these principles and is integral for ensuring we have preventative measures to protect and promote our health and wellbeing. Wellbeing at work integrates physical and mental health, so they are not thought of as standing alone or being separate; they are closely intertwined. We will introduce the concept of professional self-care that leads to a community of care for us all. When the concept of achieving work-life balance is valued and honoured, we can all apply personal and professional boundary setting that enables us to achieve more by doing less and that cultivates resilience, comfort, security, and safety.

DOI: 10.4324/9781003146247-10

HEALTH AND HARMONY

Cultivating a mentally healthy workplace environment, nurturing, and valuing resilience, promoting work-life balance through a community of care.

 Table 6.1 Health and harmony

Protective factors	Risk factors
Systems and structures empower staff to develop a healthy work-life balance – for example, leaders model good working practices and self-care to encourage an appropriate work-life balance.	There is little care, thought, or attention to the health and wellbeing of staff or regard to the benefits of promoting a healthy lifestyle.
• Staff to take breaks in suitable and comfortable spaces. • There are suitable private and comfortable spaces for staff to undertake their religious practices. • Leaders and managers are respectful of cultural and religious celebrations that require fasting, such as Lent, Yom Kippur, and Ramadan. • Finishing on time is the norm. • Staff have regular debriefs or supervision from colleagues or line managers when dealing with difficult situations. • Efforts are made to review paperwork/procedures/practice to simplify and reduce workload, "achieve more with less". • There are a range of free resources that promote wellbeing in the workplace. • Nutritious meals are provided free of charge, healthy food and water is available.	• There is insufficient space for comfort, rest, breaks, and lunch away from the children. • Staff are repeatedly asked to stay late, come in early, cancel a holiday, attend meetings or training on days off. • Little consideration is giving to change, or how stressful or demanding circumstances will affect staff wellbeing. • No regard is given to staff views on paperwork or reducing workload. • Little care or respect is paid to staff's cultural and religious beliefs and how they are an important part of health and wellbeing.

Protective factors	Risk factors
Attention and care are given to the working environment in which staff work.	Staff morale and motivation is low. In extreme situations, staff health is affected.
• Consideration of the physical environment is given for neurodivergent colleagues, such as providing low arousal spaces. • Risk assessments are reviewed and completed, audits of stressors, such as flickering lights, loud noises, low temperature are carried out. • Stress surveys are completed, and results and actions are followed up. • There is a trained staff member who has completed a physical first aid course for adults.	• Staff work long hours in unsuitable and uncomfortable spaces. • No thought or care is given to given to learning differences and adaptations that would support staff with physical or mental health issues. • Stress is not addressed, and it impacts staff mental and physical health and presentism and absenteeism.
Line managers understand and advocate the importance of mental health awareness and have completed training.	There is a lack of care and understanding towards mental health
• All staff have had training on mental health awareness and know the early warning signs of mental ill-health. • There are named mental health first aiders. • Named wellbeing champions to promote days and weeks of the year, signpost local and national charities, and organisations to promote health and prioritise wellbeing. • Staff enjoy professional development opportunities that relate to their wellbeing. • There are pathways in place that signpost staff access to support their health and wellbeing and invest in employee assistance programmes (EAP), human resources (HR), occupational health.	• There are no practices that emphasise preventive and protective factors for wellbeing. • Intervention is reactionary, often when a person has reached burnout, illness, crisis, or diagnosis.

SPACE FOR REFLECTION

Which protective factors do you identify with?   Which risk factors do you identify with?

What evidence do I have for protective factors within my setting?

Mental health first aid

We all have a part to play; nobody should be one conversation away from the help and support they need.

I trained to become a Mental Health First Aid (MHFA) England instructor in 2018, as I wanted to provide appropriate training, with the idea that we need all of the skills that can prevent mental health issues from worsening, provide early intervention, and signpost for support. Something that I felt could help me and many others I know. Mental Health First Aid is an evidence research-based training programme and global community that raises mental health awareness in twenty-five countries worldwide.

MHFA is a training course which teaches people how to identify, understand, and help someone who may be experiencing a mental health issue.

- MHFA won't teach you to be a therapist, but it will teach you to listen, reassure, and respond, even in a crisis – and even potentially stop a crisis from happening.
- You'll learn to recognise warning signs of mental ill-health and develop the skills and confidence to approach and support someone while keeping yourself safe.
- You'll also learn how to empower someone to access the support they might need for recovery or successful management of symptoms. This could include self-help books or websites, accessing therapy services through their GP, their school or place of work, online self-referral, support groups, and more.
- What's more, you'll gain an understanding of how to support positive wellbeing and tackle stigma in the world around you.

(MHFA England, 2021)

 RACHEL AND FRAN'S STORY

In January 2020, Rachel and I had the pleasure of taking part in some mental health first aid training. To say we were inspired was the world's biggest understatement. We couldn't wait to get back to our teams and implement all we had learned. We had staff at both our nurseries who we had already supported through some mental health challenges, and they were our first beneficiaries of our training. We created well-ness support plans that were tailored to each individual. This gave us a great opportunity to spend some quality time with each staff member and ensure we knew exactly how to help them and positively support their mental health. We set up techniques to check in and we also implemented plans to ensure that no staff member became overwhelmed. Each staff member is supported individually – the same approach we would take with each child and family that comes to our nurseries. Whenever a new staff member joins our teams, we always promote this so everyone knows we will be there to support them through whatever life throws at us. It isn't just a team – it's a family.

The introduction of wellbeing Wednesdays across the nurseries was a huge success and the team enjoyed taking on some of the techniques we learned. We introduced the "happiness hour" each week and promoted "self-care" as much as possible. The teams thrived and we saw them putting themselves first and enjoyed sharing pictures of what made them happy. As managers it also gave us great opportunities to get to know our staff on a deeper level – knowing what makes your team happy helps you to motivate and drive them. It also gave us a great opportunity to role model and ensure we were looking after ourselves. One of the biggest lessons we learnt on that training was to look after ourselves so we could look after other people.

For the first time in both our management careers we were also taking some well-deserved "me" time, and the team benefited greatly from this technique too.

Anyone who works in early years will know that it's the best job you can have – "inspiring children to change tomorrow's world" is an honour. However, no matter how inspiring it is, it can also be stressful and sometimes this stress can overwhelm you, and sometimes overtake your life. The introduction of the stress container was something we implemented with all our staff. It was especially helpful when supporting our leadership team. We found out what might stress them and set up techniques to empty that container as and when needed. This was also used at team meetings to evaluate strengths and development areas for the nurseries, allowing us to constantly thrive and develop.

Wellbeing is well and truly embedded in our practice and something that has aided us towards success. Some of our biggest success stories at both nurseries have come from the support we have implemented through the wellbeing programme.

In March 2020, the world went into lockdown and our nurseries had to close their doors. We hosted weekly wellbeing zooms with our staffing team, quizzes, karaoke nights, exercise sessions, cooking classes; available for all to keep in touch with our team throughout a very difficult time. Some of our team members lived alone, away from their families at such a scary time.

We have continued to have wellbeing at the forefront of our practice, the top of our priorities in our settings, and I really believe it is embedded in our daily practice. Mental health is a part of everyone's life, we all experience both positive and negative periods throughout our journey in life. What's important is the people around you are aware of the signs and know how to encourage and support you to take steps to feel better.

Some of our top tips from us:

1. Being a manager can be both hectic and lonely; ensure you have a fellow manager that can be aware of the signs that you may be struggling and what they can do to support you. Francesca and I work very closely to support each other's wellbeing, as well as supporting each other as managers. It's important to have someone who can recognise that your wellbeing may be declining, and she knows what makes me feel better in myself! You need to look after you to ensure you can look after so many others!

2. Encourage staff members to engage in the process, starting with wellbeing chats, offer them the opportunity to complete a wellbeing action plan; if they are overwhelmed or stressed, use the stress container exercise.

3. Challenge the staffing team to weekly or monthly challenges to encourage positive wellbeing, e.g. collectively aim to achieve a step challenge goal, book clubs, happiness hours etc.

4. Making it part of your setting's culture that you accept and support everyone; the diversity amongst a staffing team brings an

opportunity for learning, acceptance, and support. You will soon see that people will start to invest in each other more, as well as themselves. We also include wellbeing as part of our weekly email updates, staff meetings, inset days, and a termly internal newsletter, where we encourage staff members to contribute what they find helpful to support their positive mental health and wellbeing.

Rachel Cannon is an Operations Manager and Francesca Evans a Nursery Manager; they share their approach to wellbeing through visits and writing and blogs.

Stress at work

Thinking back on what we have learned about stress, it is essential to under-stand what may cause stress in our job role and consider what we are doing about it.

The Health and Safety Executive (HSE) defines work-related stress as "the adverse reaction people have to excessive pressures or other types of demand placed on them".

There are six main areas of work design that can affect stress levels. They are:

- **Demands** – this includes issues such as workload, work patterns, and the work environment
- **Control** – how much say the person has in the way they do their work
- **Support** – this includes the encouragement, sponsorship, and resources provided by the organisation, line management, and colleagues
- **Relationships** – this includes promoting positive working to avoid con-flict and dealing with unacceptable behaviour
- **Role** – whether people understand their role within the organisation and whether the organisation ensures that they do not have conflicting roles
- **Change** – how organisational change (large or small) is managed and communicated in the organisation

Taking steps to identify, reduce, and manage stress related to the six main areas of work design will positively impact everyone. Recognising signs of stress in the workplace is beneficial to everyone, especially when working with babies and children. It might seem obvious, but we still need to point out that caregivers that are not experiencing emotional, physical, mental, and social stress or stressors will be happier and healthier and, therefore, more productive at work.

Looking at the six main areas that affect work design, notice how they are incorporated into our philosophy of wellbeing. The risk factors in the health and harmony section highlight how work design is integral to protecting wellbeing at work.

Emotional agility

Developing our emotional intelligence is key to working with children today and the key to happier and healthier workplaces, professional relationships with colleagues, and job satisfaction. For example, someone asks us how we feel, and let us say, we reply, stressed! True, what might be happening in our bodies is that stress response, threatening to fire up, but we have not identified the real underlying reason for the stress response.

Interestingly, psychologist and author of *Emotional Agility* (2016), Susan David, shares her perspective on stress. It is particularly relevant to our stressed-out workforce; so often, we use an umbrella term to describe how we feel. So, when someone asks us how we are, we might say, stressed, when what we mean is frustrated. For example, just like earlier on, where we talked about stress and throwing the word around a lot and experiencing stress contagion, we become stuck in that feeling. Sisters Emily and Amelia Nagoski, authors of *Burnout* (2020), discuss how we get stuck in the stress cycle if we do not adequately deal with stress. Many of us are stuck in the stress cycle, but we are also using the word stress as an umbrella term for the issues we are not correctly dealing with. Developing our emotional agility enables us to name and deal with the *experience or situation causing the stress*. When we name it, we can take steps to tame it! "Dealing with your stress is a separate process from dealing with the things that cause you stress. To deal with your stress, you have to complete the stress cycle" (Nagoski & Nagoski, 2020).

Let me explain. If a colleague at work kept coming into work late every day, just by a few minutes, let us say; but we know just how much of a difference those few minutes can make! Maybe you do not quite know how to say something to them, and perhaps you do not even realise just how much it is beginning to bother you. Then you have a doctor's appointment and let them know you will be in slightly later than usual. When you come into work, there is an atmosphere. Your work colleague explains that your manager was not happy because parents were waiting outside when they got in because they were, as usual, a few minutes late. You explain that you had told them you would be in late today, but it feels like this is now your fault, which feels frustrating and unfair. What is the real issue here? The real issue is that you have a problem with a colleague at work and you do not know how to go about it. It is really starting to bother how you feel at work.

Have you experienced anything similar?

 ## ADDRESS YOUR STRESS

When stress shows up in our bodies, what do we do about it? Stress is not the cause; it is the symptom and result of a situation or experience.

When we can identify the proper understanding of why you feel this way and identify the root cause, we can take steps to address it. Connecting our emotions – thoughts and feelings – to how we feel physically; noticing sensations and how these influence and affect our behaviour and actions.

What do I find stressful at work?
What existing stress may need my attention right now?
What new stress am I aware of?
How can my workplace support me right now?
How can I support myself right now?
Do I work with someone who is stressed and anxious?
Do I work with someone who is calm?

Resilience

Resilience is another word that we hear a lot. We might know resilience as that bounce-back ability. But do we all naturally have resilience? The answer is no – that age-old nature versus nurture debate. Even though we think of resilience as bouncing back, we tend to think that means we always remain strong, or keep on going, no matter what. Think back to times that have been challenging and complex and the occasions where you made mistakes and failed. Perhaps you notice that these are the times when you actually learnt the most. Resilience is about learning to bend, not break.

I remember my daughter, who was around eleven or twelve at the time, was competing in a school athletics competition with all schools from the local area. She was competing in the high jump, and even though she tried her best, she did not make it past the first round and did not manage to jump a height that she had usually jumped easily. Understandably she felt upset and disappointed. Her next event was running the third leg in the relay race! No pressure. She was adamant that she did not want to do it. In fact, she felt she could not do it. There might have even been some tears, but do not tell her I said that. She felt like there was no point even trying, as she was so worried she was going to let the whole team down I encouraged her to try her best. They lined up at their starting positions. The whistle went off. The girls started and from where I was in the sports arena, I could not quite see them coming round the bend. When someone did emerge, legging it and in the lead about to pass the baton, it was my daughter! I held my breath as she passed on the baton. They only went and won the relay race!

I promise it really was as exciting as it sounds. For weeks and now years later, we still talk about that day how we both learnt something about failing and wanting to give up. The fact that she failed the first time and tried again made that relay victory all the more thrilling and rewarding. That those funny feelings in our tummy are sometimes there to keep us safe, but also have the power to stop us from potential joy and future accomplishments, and even doing those scary things that we do not yet know that we are good at! Resilience is described by the psychologist Ann Masten as "ordinary magic", resilience is not always the big relay races in life. Sometimes it is getting out of bed in the morning and putting one foot in front of another. Failing and trying repeatedly, and finding the feeling even sweeter, making mistakes, and learning from it for the future. To discover our own ordinary magic, we need someone to support and encourage us, but we also need to believe in ourselves. To promote resilience in the spaces that we occupy, specifically thinking of how we develop a community of care within our EY ecosystems that cultivates encouragement, nurtures, and tends to our needs to quietly create our own magic and resilience so that we can all thrive.

In Chapter 2, on mental health, we looked at signs and symptoms of mental health issues. Take a look at the following case study and use the information you have learnt, and the risk and protective factors, to answer the questions.

Case study reflection

Let us look at a hypothetical case study example that we can use to apply the risk and protective factors to identify and address wellbeing issues.

Noreen is a staff member you have known for about three years; you started working as TAs at the same time, so you have always shared a bond. You get along well and enjoy sharing your lunch breaks together. They have recently moved from nursery into reception and are working with a new teacher, who is the EYFS phase leader. They were excited at this new role and learning new skills with a different age group.

However, Noreen has started avoiding the staff room at lunchtime. They do not pop in and say hello and catch up with you like they once did. You heard two reception teachers talking about how Noreen "was off work again". Next time you see Noreen in the staff meeting, they look like they have lost weight and do not contribute in the way they usually do and rushes out as soon as the meeting ends. Noreen is usually helpful in organising end-of-term jobs, and you notice they seem unsure and hesitant about making decisions. When you have to pop into the reception class to collect something, you notice Noreen responds to how the EYFS Phase leader speaks to them.

You are starting to feel a little worried about Noreen and are not quite sure what to do about it. You decide to mention it to the head-teacher. They tell you that you are not the first to mention concerns about Noreen and her change in performance. The following week you see Noreen coming out of the headteacher's office, and she is visibly upset. They tell you that people have been complaining about them not pulling their weight and doing as well in reception as they thought. You feel terrible because you never intended for this to happen.

What do you say to Noreen?
What could have been done differently?
What can you do to support Noreen?
What signs and symptoms of mental health issues do you see?
What might be stopping Noreen from asking for help or talking to you?

Let us think about it this way: thinking about the signs and symptoms we can see certainly indicates a change in Noreen. Some emotional, physical, and behavioural signs indicate Noreen's mental wellbeing has changed. You clearly care about Noreen, but something has stopped you from directly asking her if she is okay. Suppose you had felt able to speak to Noreen directly. In that case, this may have meant that whatever Noreen is dealing with right now could have been addressed through an informal check-in, showing that you care and are always around to listen, rather than what must have felt like a formal discussion on work-related issues with the headteacher.

Put yourself in Noreen's shoes: you have been working in a school for three years. When you find the new role and line manager difficult and challenging, they email over the weekend with planning for each new week. You begin to dread coming to work, waking up on Sunday night overthinking the week ahead, feeling stressed a lot of the time, and starting to pick up bugs, and coughs and colds, and feeling really run down. You are trying to hold everything together and do the best you can in a job that you used to love. When your headteacher pulls you in for a formal discussion, you feel embarrassed, and think people must have been talking about you. You wonder why if everyone felt this way that nobody said anything. You feel defensive because up until now, you have never had any issues at work. You feel like everyone is against you and wonder why everything that you have been struggling with is being said to you in a way that makes you feel that you are letting people down, and actually not very good at your job after all.

- How would you feel if this happened to you or someone that you loved?
- What could you do now?
- What can you do to support Noreen?

Seeing people as people, not just a resource. If the first port of call we use to check in on someone comes from a perspective of "you are not doing your job properly", it would feel like nobody cares about you. They just care about the job. When we see people as people and not just a resource, a number, or a ratio, then we are placing that person at the heart, we are saying your health matters first.

Thinking about ways to check in with someone, like, "you haven't seemed yourself lately, I miss seeing you at lunchtime" or "fancy a cuppa after work" or "shall we go for a walk at lunchtime", so that you are thinking about the right time and place, you are showing you genuinely care.

 Looking at the protective factors for health and harmony, what things might have made a difference in Noreen's case – had they been in place?

Professional self-care leads to a community of care

Let us consider how professional self-care is essential for us all but often overlooked. Professional self-care is ultimately about the boundaries that we put in place to safeguard our health and wellbeing, enabling us to be more effective in our roles. In this day and age, we try to do all of the things, for all of the people, all of the time. Working in EY is as challenging and exhausting as it is rewarding and satisfying. We blur the lines between work, rest, and play. We set ourselves up to fail. We cannot possibly do all the things for all of the people if we are not doing anything for ourselves. We can do it all. Just not at the same time.

The healthier and happier we feel in ourselves will translate into how we go about our day, fulfil daily duties and responsibilities, and ultimately the quality of our practice. The children you care for will get the best of you – not what is left of you!

Here are a few ways to consider how taking care of yourself will put you in the best possible position to take care of others.

Eat well – breakfast, lunch, and tea. Skipping breakfast only makes us hungry, our energy levels dip, and we feel less productive. Lunch breaks are not a treat or a one-off special occasion. They are essential. Not taking a break and wearing a badge of exhaustion does not help anyone. It probably makes you feel like you have less patience for people who demand your attention. Having a break where you can socialise with your team, rest, enables you to take a breather and refuel.

Start on time, finish on time. If our job role requires us to consistently work hours above and beyond our contracted hours, then something is not right with either the work design or the number of responsibilities you have for your role. I am not trying to oversimplify it. I understand this can be exceedingly difficult to address and manage. There are many reasons why we may find ourselves starting early and finishing late, some within our control and some outside of control. Especially when you work with children, there may be occasions when you may have to stay over due to staffing or unexpected events. If this happens regularly, then this needs to be addressed. If you have a leadership role, then when you model how it is important to finish on time, you are showing everyone else to prioritise this. If not, you may be unknowingly creating a culture that expects and demands more. That includes emails – do not send, read, and reply unless it is within usual working hours. Have you ever had an email over the weekend or late at night, that as soon as you have read it, causes you a great deal of worry, anxiety, or even panic? I have, I used to receive emails from my line manager at all hours of the day and night, and because I was new to my role and eager to make a good impression, I made myself constantly available. This made me constantly available to pressure, critique, and meant I never switched off from work.

Think about what this does to our stress response. It means we continually exist in a state of fear, threat detection systems ready to jump into action. Take emails off your phone so you are not alerted. You cannot be at the beck and call of families, colleagues or anyone 24/7. Set up timings so that your emails go out within working hours, write in your email signature the hours that you work and how long it may take for people to expect a reply. This puts your mind at ease and the people who are contacting you. Likewise, when you go on holiday or are having a particularly busy period, set up an automated email response letting people know you are on holiday, provide dates when you will return, and who they should contact in an emergency.

Work. **Life**. **Balance**. Your job and the career that you work so hard for is a big part of who you are. However, it should not be all of who you are. Truth be told, not every single person that works with children has that intrinsic wiring, maybe it is not their special talent, yet we need a job, and so we have to work. We seem to expect so much from ourselves and each other, especially when considering the wages of any early years educator. Our salary comparative to other professions is low. How do you, as a lone worker, or as a team member, incorporate work, life, balance into your working environment? Not every training session or staff meeting has to be about Ofsted, observations, assessments, and children's progress. Whether you work alone or in a team, what needs your attention right now regarding health and harmony – extend that culture of kindness to yourself.

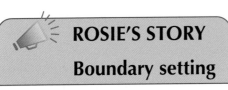

ROSIE'S STORY
Boundary setting

Learning where my boundaries lay as a childminder was one of the most significant learning curves that I went through after I started. Because the job is undertaken from our home, the implications on the rest of my family, but also our family time and "space" were things that had to be tweaked as we went along.

There is no way of knowing when you start out, how your own children (if you have them) will respond to sharing their parent's attention and their space and things. There is no way of knowing what hours you will find become "too much". There is no way of knowing how well the parents you take on will understand your role and the relationship that you need to have to work positively together.

These things took time to untangle and sometimes that took getting messages whilst on holiday, or at 10 pm at night on a Saturday, before realising my boundaries and learning to communicate them positively. The pandemic highlighted for many the magnitude at which we are valued by some and not by others and that for many childminders gave space to consider new boundaries. Suddenly, during the pandemic the lines between "work" and "home" became even more blurred and in order to create a sense of more control it was necessary to reconsider lots of things such as new working hours or policies and procedures.

I found the biggest change for me overall in managing my boundaries was being super clear prior to visits, during visits, and in the follow up to visits, how my business ran. That meant troubleshooting all the potential boundary crossing that might arise later on that we can find tricky, stressful, and difficult to confront. For example, being very clear about sickness policies or your pay policy from the start allows parents to see that you have clear expectations and policies in place. This is much easier than chasing for payment or having conversations about misunderstandings over bank holidays or a parent arriving on your doorstep with a sick child.

Communication really is key; having a friendly and open relationship with families whilst also maintaining boundaries, ultimately keeps everybody feeling secure. Letting parents know that you don't answer your phone over the weekend unless it is an emergency, lets them value you and your family time. Just because you work from home, it does not mean that you and your home are always accessible. Those boundaries are key to your mental health and wellbeing, and also the wellbeing of your family, who also need to see that they are not always second in the pecking order.

Rosie Joyce

PROFESSIONAL SELF-CARE
Setting your own boundaries

What needs my attention at work right now?
What support do I need to put in boundaries at work?
How often do I take a lunch break or allow time for rest/organise my day (if I am a nanny or childminder)?
Do the meals I eat sustain and fulfil me, providing me with the energy I need to do my role?

Early years wellness plan

The Wellness Recovery Action Plan® or WRAP®, was developed by Dr Mary Ellen Copeland and is a self-designed prevention and wellness process that anyone can use to get well, stay well, and make their life the way they want it to be. Originally for people experiencing mental health issues, it is now used extensively by people navigating all kinds of circumstances to support them to reach their full potential and provide support with physical, mental health and life issues.

Given the often high levels of stress in the workplace and the increased number of staff reporting mental health issues, a wellness plan, if implemented effectively, will support all staff to manage their mental health and wellbeing at work. The idea is that staff develop their own personalised tool that they can use to help them stay well and address health issues as they arise. It enables open, honest, and clear communication between line managers and their team. Think carefully about how you introduce this to staff and decide on how and when you will complete it and how often it will be reviewed. Keep it as simple as possible. We do not need the pressure of unnecessary paperwork, but providing staff with the tools and necessary information about why it is helpful to complete one, is an additional measure to maintain and protect wellbeing.

YOUR PERSONALISED WELLNESS PLAN

Do I have any pre-existing or diagnosed health conditions or any other health issues?

Do I take any medication?

What do I need to do every day to stay well or keep on track with my goals?

What helps me stay healthy?

What am I like when I am well?

What do I wish my manager knew?

What do I wish I could explain to my colleagues?

How can my workplace support me right now?
Are there any situations that may trigger poor mental health?
How do I want to feel as I navigate this situation and maintain my wellness?
What can I do to take care of the things that are worrying me?
How does work positively contribute to my overall wellness?

An intersectional approach to wellbeing

COMMUNITY CARE IN ACTION

What would you value in your workplace that would enable you to develop a community of care?
What are you already doing well?
What could be improved?
Think about a community of care in the form of people and their actions and behaviours, systems – what are the policies and procedures that protect, safeguard?

STRENGTHENING SELF-CARE TO LEAD US TO VALUE COMMUNITY CARE

Knowing that working in EY can be stressful and demanding, what do you do to take care of yourself?
How do we look out for each other in the workplace?
How do we seek to understand and value cultural beliefs and experiences of self-care?
How is community care developed through self-care?

Take a moment to talk about other things that we do not talk openly about.

Health issues we need to talk more about

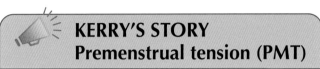

KERRY'S STORY
Premenstrual tension (PMT)

We work in a female-dominated environment, yet discussing menstruation still seems so taboo.

There have been countless occasions where I have had to deal with my dreaded period when caring for young children, and I have always just sucked it up because I am a woman, and period pains are part of life. Like many women, I have been conditioned to believe that pain is something I must accept, and with the prevalence of health conditions such as endometriosis, we are largely expected to leave our baggage at the door. Unfortunately, we cannot leave our vaginas at the door and so we need to start talking openly about the occupational impact of menstruation, menopause, and vaginal health.

Periods can come early, when you are without painkillers, and we all know that if you don't catch it in time, it leads to full-blown agony. To not be able to ask for help in that moment because of societal expectations for us to soldier on, is not right. Children are wonderful, but they are literally the worst remedy for a period ache that you feel from your fingertips to your toes.

Menstruation is an ongoing feature of our lives, affecting our hormones, moods, emotional states, and behaviours. Periods don't just impact us in the week we are "on" but are operating in the background across the whole month. For example, in the ten days prior to my period, I have sensitive and swollen breasts, and I literally need to socially distance from anyone coming near them because they are so painful. And you guessed it, children jumping in for hugs is triggering and uncomfortable. Each person has a set of physiological and psychological symptoms that they must manage, and within all of this, we carry shame and embarrassment because, again, society creates a narrative that periods are dirty. If we dare to express our menstrual experiences, we are accused of being "due-on" and therefore unstable, or we are giving too much information. We are subjected to language that degrades us "she's on the rag" and we are silenced.

There are several issues we must address in the early years:

1. Menstruation is a continuous cycle, and so we need to consider how we support people in the different stages of their cycle across a month. For example, "I know you get a sore back when you are on your period, so I can do some more of the lifting today".
2. It is not only women who have periods, and we should not make that assumption. A "period positive" workplace welcomes anyone with a period to share their needs and to have them met, as per our occupational health policies.
3. We should not perpetuate harmful stereotypes about menstruation and periods, and we should be open and unapologetic for openly talking about our needs.
4. Menstruation is part of our menstruation life cycle.
5. Period poverty is prevalent within our workforces, and we need to recognise that people may face additional challenges trying to manage their period. For example, do not assume that staff can afford sanitary products, many cannot. Signpost to charities and organisations or provide these as part of occupational health.
6. Ethical period products are a privilege item. Do not judge people who do not opt for egg cups, period underwear or ethical brands.

Our workplace being "period positive" is crucial if we are to thrive at work. The adverts have led us to believe that periods are clean, straightforward, and empowering. I can confirm I have never worn a white tennis skirt on my period or rode a wild stallion. Keeping my sanitary towel from doing a twister as I walk down the street is challenge enough.

Ways to be "period positive".

- Acknowledge that menstruation is not an excuse. This is not an episode of *Grange Hill*. We are not trying to avoid P.E. lessons.

- Premenstrual tension (PMT) often inflates what we are feeling but it doesn't mean that we don't still feel it when we don't have PMT. I always call PMT my "spidey-sense" – it is the time of the month where my deeper emotional grievances rear their heads giving me chance to plan to address them when my mood stabilises. If a member of staff says, "I am just due-on", let them know that their feelings are still valid if they want to talk about it at another time.
- Talk openly and non-ashamedly about menstruation and menopause. If you are comfortable, explain if there are additional health conditions.
- Put together a "period positive policy", which clearly outlines your stance on periods. We must acknowledge that periods come with additional burdens, for example, period poverty. A policy is also important to demonstrate to employers that vaginal care is important.
- I advise that settings do offer "period breaks" because the blood loss during a period leads to lower energy levels and increased fatigue. A sweet tea goes a long way during those moments and encouraging staff to stretch it out before going into their classrooms is a slight but powerful habit for getting rid of anxious tension.
- As well as a policy, there is also an opportunity to have some basic period positive provisions, for example, having a hot water bottle in the staff room, stocking some pain-relief and herbal tea bags. Could staff bathrooms include a few sanitary products, and self-care products? Periods can be heavy, so if a staff member gets the unexpected visitor, it's good to know they can access these things.

I am going to end on two period anecdotes – a serious and funny one.

Serious

Growing up, I lived in poverty and having a period was quite literally my worst nightmare. In a house of three women, we did not have a regular supply of sanitary products and I have made towels out of lots of different items, because when you live in poverty, you have to get creative. My mum eventually got a free supply of Tena ladies for an incontinence issue and throughout my teenage years, that's what I had to use. Let's just say, they don't deal with blood as well as they do with urine. Periods, whether we like it or not, come with shame, and had I experienced a "period positive" culture, my view of menstruation may be very different. While it is not our job to fix everything for our staff, we know that for our workforce, there are vulnerabilities and if we can make it a little easier why wouldn't we?

Funny (and mortifying)

I recently wore a skirt when visiting my in-laws. When I got there, I definitely had a sanitary towel on, but when I left, I suddenly realised it must have fallen out somewhere. So, my parting gift was a used, scrunched up sanitary towel that must have been discovered somewhere. Safe to say it has never been mentioned, but that is life sometimes. We cannot live in the shadows of our ovaries.

www.seeherthrive.com/blog/2020/8/26/how-to-create-a-period-friendly-workplace-and-why-its-crucial-to-company
https://periodpoverty.uk/

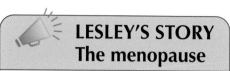

LESLEY'S STORY
The menopause

Sixteen years ago, when I was 34 years old, we were told that we could not have children. When I collapsed at work and was rushed to hospital with suspected meningitis, I found out I was pregnant with our gorgeous daughter who is now 15, "Love of my life".

Fast forward six years when I hit 40 and I thought my whole health and wellbeing were falling apart. It was not until I was 46 that I was finally told that I was going through the menopause. Six years I survived thinking I was losing my mind until after numerous visits, I went to my GP and begged them to believe me something was not right and said that someone had to help me. Finally, I started HRT, and it made me feel semi-human again! Believe me, it did not remove all the signs and symptoms, but it made me feel that I could live again as normally as I could.

Working in the early years, I am going to make a very sweeping statement and say much of the workforce are women. What support do women get going through at the latter stage of our lives to cope with the menopause? It is getting better but is there still a lack of understanding. Many women struggle and end up leaving their employment due to lack of support and understanding. Working in Scotland there is a major recruitment crisis for early years workers and with the increase in free childcare hours coming in, 11,000 more practitioners are needing to be recruited. Is there a generation of ladies being overlooked?

Since being told that I am going through the full-blown menopause with the help of HRT, it has not all been a bed of roses. I managed five services, and now only three. I work for a charity, who do amazing work, but at times it is challenging. I was managing all my symptoms well, had so much support in the office and was open and honest when I was having a not so great day. I was totally and utterly devastated when I was told by my then line manager at my appraisal, that with all that I manage and deal with there was one day she said that she heard me come out of my office and say, "I am so menopausal" and apparently stomped up the corridor. I must admit that I have no recollection of doing this ... but this could be due to the memory loss that I have too!!

This one statement really affected me in a way that is hard to explain. Had I, did I, why was this just being brought up at my appraisal? I stopped speaking about what I was feeling, how I was coping as I thought I was being judged on my performance at work. My team noticed that there had been a change, and they absolutely rallied around to support and help me.

Then my daughter asked me to start doing the Couch to 5K running plan. Never in my life did I think that I would run or be able to run five kilometres. My health is the best it has been for years, my mental wellbeing is clearer and more focused than ever, and it's all thanks to running.

We are looking after families' most precious beings, but we also need to look after ourselves, for us to be 100 per cent able to care and educate our future generation – they have a lot of responsibility on their shoulders. Remember you are just as important, and you are a significant part of our children's lives so please think of your health and wellbeing as a number one priority.

Lesley Tait, Head of Childcare Services
https://menopausesupport.co.uk/
www.cipd.co.uk/knowledge/culture/well-being/menopause
www.nhs.uk/conditions/menopause/

How will you know your protective factors develop a mentally healthy working environment that prides itself on resilience and a community of care

How will you know your protective factors contribute towards a mentally healthy workplace culture?

You will see how the core values promote the protective factors and bring them to life. Staff are happy, healthy, and well supported. Core values are visible in the everyday actions of the whole community.

As a team and/or in collaboration with families, discuss what a resilient community of care would look, feel, and sound like in everyday practice. What does mentally healthy mean to us? What would this require from leaders and staff? What would the impact be on staff, children, families, and the quality of the overall provision? Choose your own unique setting, specific behaviours or characteristics. I have given some examples in Figure 6.1.

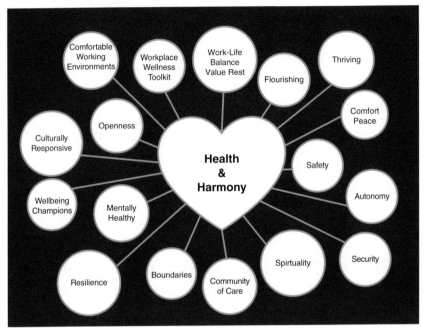

Figure 6.1 Health and harmony

 **FINAL THOUGHTS**

Workplace wellness toolkit

See pages 89–90 for a reminder of some ideas to create your own.

Have you identified any actions in the 'Core value: health and harmony' section that need your attention?

References

David, S. (2017). *Emotional Agility: Get Unstuck, Embrace Change, and Thrive in Work and Life.* London: Penguin.

Health and Safety Executive (HSE). (n.d.) Stress and mental health at work. Managing stress at work. Available at: https://www.hse.gov.uk/stress/

Masten, A.S. (2015). *Ordinary Magic: Resilience in Development.* Guilford Press.

MHFA England. (2021). Available at: https://mhfaengland.org/individuals/adult/

Nagoski, E. and Nagoski, A. (2020). *Burnout: The Secret to Unlocking the Stress Cycle.* New York: Ballantine Books.

The Wellness Recovery Action Plan® or WRAP® Available at: https://copelandcenter.com/wellness-recovery-action-plan-wrap

A culture of kindness and accountability

Exploring core values

This core value introduces us to a culture of kindness and accountability. Does your workplace help or hinder staff wellbeing? For example, we know our EY ecosystem is cultivated through its community. So how well the setting is consistently organised and operated will depend on how effective EYE are in their roles, their everyday actions, behaviour, and the attitude of all the team. The relational environment – how staff professional and personal relationships are nurtured – will be cultivated through your philosophy, ethos, and underpinning core values and beliefs.

The role of an EYE means hours are especially long, and the role demands a lot. When working such long hours with few breaks, it is essential to feel that the colleagues we share all our days and hours with care about us, respect us, and treat us kindly. This chapter will focus on the critical and necessary skills of being emotionally intelligent practitioners – so we have the empathy and emotional literacy to develop our roles as caregivers and develop our relationships with others.

The Ofsted education inspection framework (EIF) report asks, "What is it like to be a child in this setting?" Instead, we will consider *what is it like to be a member of staff in this setting?*

DOI: 10.4324/9781003146247-11

Why did we choose the role we do and the setting we work in? And now that we are thinking about it, how does it *feel* to work here? Is the culture mentally healthy? Do I feel valued and respected? How do we speak to, treat, and take care of each other? Use the risk and protective factors to reflect on your practice and the ethos within your own setting.

CULTURE OF KINDNESS AND ACCOUNTABILITY

Emotionally intelligent leaders and educators work with intention, developing trust, cooperation, respect, and dignity.

 Table 7.1 Culture of kindness and accountability

Protective factors	Risk factors
All staff complete training on self-regulation and emotional intelligence, and this is recognised as a core value. • Emotional intelligent leadership cultivates relationships, communication and trust. • Staff are supported to self-regulate.	Leaders and staff members who cannot self-regulate their emotions. • There is a fear and worry of getting things wrong and a view that things have to be perfect, and an attitude that there is no room for mistakes. • Staff and leaders lack self-awareness, and this affects relationships, communication, and trust.
Line managers have received training and ongoing support to enable them to develop the necessary skills to facilitate and lead meaningful performance management. • Staff trust in the systems that are in place for performance management and see results that support personal and professional development. • Time, care, and privacy is given to the organisation of performance management meetings.	Line managers have not received or completed little professional development relating to performance management, including induction. • Line managers that complete performance management are ill-equipped to deal with staff issues sensitively. • Staff lack respect and are uncooperative and do not trust in the systems in place to support them. • Performance management is a tick-box exercise, ineffectual, and does not make any impact on staff practice.

Protective factors	Risk factors
• Staff dignity is considered in all systems, structures, and paperwork; when additional support and adaptations are identified, staff trust in the process. • Disciplinaries and discussions relating to staff and their code of conduct are dealt with respectfully and follow policy and procedures in a timely manner, fairly, and consistently. • Staff are accountable for their actions.	• Staff are apathetic towards any form of performance management and openly lack motivation. • Line managers do not model their own accountability in everyday practice. • Staff are not held accountable for breaches of policy and procedure, and the quality of provision is low and breaches welfare requirements.
Staff views, thoughts, and feelings are valued and regularly sought to measure job satisfaction, performance, and wellbeing to identify elements of practice, policy or culture that may be detrimental to a healthy work-life balance. • Staff questionnaires, wellbeing surveys and or any methods that encourage staff to share their views. • Staff views continually evaluate and update on practice, such as policies and procedures. • Staff feel comfortable and confident to talk about issues that arise, and trust line managers will do the right thing by them.	Staff lack confidence in line managers as there is little effort to engage with them in meaningful ways. For example, they do not seek staff views, so the whole team's ideas are not considered and do not improve performance. • Staff lack trust in line managers, as failures to address issues that arise have led to further conflict.
A team manifesto and staff handbook developed by all of the staff community supports the development and skill of emotionally intelligent practice and relationships. • Staff bring their whole selves to work, and the workplace benefits from all of the characteristics and talents that make staff members unique.	There are no formal agreements or expectations of how staff speak, treat, and work with one another. • This leads to disputes, wellbeing issues, and disharmony. • Staff hide away huge parts of their identity, and the workplace is poorer because of it. • Staff lived experiences are denied or ignored, and this leads to gaslighting.

SPACE FOR REFLECTION

Which protective factors do you identify with?

Which risk factors do you identify with?

What evidence do I have for protective factors within my setting?

Case study reflection

Let us look at a hypothetical case study example that we can use to apply the risk and protective factors to identify and address wellbeing issues.

A CULTURE OF A PARANOIA

Jenny has been working as a teaching assistant in a nursery class for 16 months. When her five-year-old daughter is unwell with tonsillitis, Jenny has to take two days off work. Her daughter has been ill for a week and already been seen by the doctor. Whilst off work, Jenny posts a Facebook status saying how relieved she is that her daughter has antibiotics. When Jenny returns to work, she can feel there is an uncomfortable atmosphere. She has to pop and ask the headteacher a question, and the headteacher is quite short with her response and says she does not have time right now. The following week in a whole team staff meeting, the headteacher reminds staff that if they are off work sick, even if it is with their children, they are not permitted to make Facebook posts. Jenny feels humiliated. Everyone in the staff room knows that this is about her. Jenny feels so upset and now realises that she had done something wrong, and the senior leadership team were not happy with her. Over time there are other occasions where Jenny feels frozen out, and she starts to feel increasingly paranoid and anxious. She never really knows where she stands with the leadership team. Emails are regularly sent out of hours, and over the weekend. Jenny feels pressure to read, reply, and respond because sometimes this is when performance feedback is shared. She never knows where she stands, and it is starting to affect her confidence and she is developing a lack of trust in her line managers.

- What is the real issue here?
- Thinking about the protective factors, what could support Jenny and her line managers?
- Does my line manager understand how their decisions and behaviours affect how others feel at work?
- Is my line manager good at helping others feel better when they are disappointed or upset?
- If I am a line manager, are there things that I avoid or put off doing?

Listening to our EY ecosystem, what can you hear?

Have you ever just stopped and listened to what your EY environment sounds like? Have you felt the gentle hum and rhythm of your community going about their daily EY lives and paused to listen to what educators say and how children speak? Our spaces are like an echo chamber, and the way we think and feel about ourselves translates into the language that we use, not only for our inner dialogue but the way we speak to and about others. After all, we shape the vocabulary and communication of our very youngest, from babies to preschoolers; modelling and practising as they form and say their very first sounds and words. The language we use and the words we speak shape the inner voice of other human beings. For example, have you ever seen a preschooler mimicking you complete the register? They repeat things you say down to the intonation and pitch of your voice and your body language? Many years ago, my team and I had some training with a wonderful local authority adviser, Sarah Bright. She taught us to think about how our EY spaces sounded and, in turn, what they felt like for us as a team, for the children in our care, and for people that visited. As a team, we reflected on the words, language, and phrases that we used and how that translated into our pedagogy and practice. Our everyday actions matter, the way we speak to each other informs the way we treat each other and vice versa, and it weaves its way into our EY eco-systems and our community.

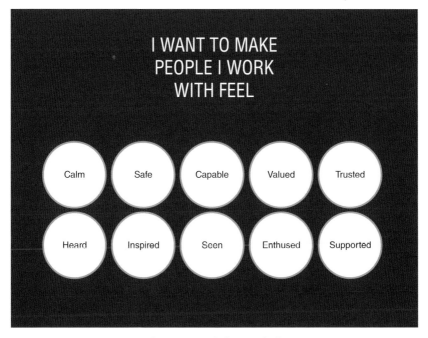

Figure 7.1 How I want people in my workplace to feel

I WANT TO MAKE PEOPLE I WORK WITH FEEL

Self-talk

"To bring out the best in others, you first need to bring out the best in yourself".

Earlier in the book, we discussed the power of our thoughts and beliefs, and shining our light. Here we will build on that and add in the power of our language. The way we think about ourselves also translates to how we speak about ourselves and our everyday language. I do not know about you, but I used to be terrible at accepting a compliment! If someone said, I like your top. I had to come back with, "oh, thanks. It was 99p from Primark. It actually has a hole in it". Sound familiar? It took a long time before I could just smile and reply with "thank you". Our everyday actions are about developing the personal, social, and emotional development of young children, but we often struggle to do this ourselves.

Early years affirmations to amplify positive emotions

Affirmations are positive phrases or statements that help us feel positively about ourselves and our talents and can challenge those thinking distortions and quiet that inner critic. They can help in aspects of life, like job interviews, exams, Ofsted inspections! We can use affirmations when we try new things and they help us with preparing ourselves mentally, emotionally, and spiritually. I first discovered affirmations through reading the book *You Are a Badass* by Jen Sincero. This is one of my favourite books of all times. I have a well-worn copy next to my bed and listen to Jen on Audible audiobook service when driving for work. The motto behind the book is that there is only one you! One uniquely special and talented you. The suggestions for the affirmations were choosing a set of phrases you can repeat to yourself in times of stress, worry or uncertainty, or at times of success. Stick these words on Post-it Notes and pop them around the place so that you can read and repeat them. I remember I was doing a really scary keynote speech, and I wrote a little Post-it Note to myself. I discovered it months and months later, after the big scary work thing. Not only did I feel well-chuffed and happy with myself as it reminded me of that scary time, but it also helped me to reread those words. In the workplace, as a team, you could write team affirmations that link to your core values, but I also highly recommend personal and private ones just for yourself; you do not have to show them to anyone, they are for only for you, in the words of Jen Sincero, there is only one you, that is your "superpower".

The "What's love got to do with it?" longitudinal study (Barside & O'Neill, 2014), shared data that supported how certain emotions have the potential to transform the workplace; with the idea that "feelings of affection, compassion, caring and tenderness for others" are valuable among colleagues, in what they call "a culture of companionate love". Indeed, in organisations where positive emotions are cultivated, they report lower levels of exhaustion, fewer sick days; "amplifying positive emotions" also reduced burnout, absenteeism, and increased commitment (Brackett, 2019).

PERSONAL AFFIRMATIONS

Such as:

- I am bright, brilliant, and beautiful
- I am brave (they do not all have to start with B)
- I am good at what I do
- I work hard
- I have good ideas
- I deserve all the good things
- I am passionate
- I am doing MY best
- I am calm and confident
- I love myself today exactly as I am
- My self-talk is loving and supportive
- I have everything I need
- I am ready for the day
- I am going to make this day count
- I am here to get it right not be right

 Can you write some of your own?

PROFESSIONAL AFFIRMATIONS

Such as:

- We find ways to work smarter, not harder
- I welcome work-life balance
- I am proud of our community
- Our community want the best for each other
- We trust and respect one another
- We encourage each other to grow
- We respect and value each other's opinions
- We are proud of our core values and the care and education we provide
- We learn through play and children are thriving in every way

How will you know your protective factors support a culture of kindness and accountability?

How will you know your protective factors contribute towards a mentally healthy workplace culture?
You will see how the core values promote the protective factors and bring them to life. Staff are thriving in emotionally intelligent relationships and trust one another. Core values are evident in everyday actions, attitudes, and interactions. Visible in the daily actions of the whole community. There is an openness for improvement and collaboration.

As a team, and/or in collaboration with families, discuss what a resilient community of care would look, feel and sound like in everyday practice? How does working in a culture of kindness and accountability matter to us? What would this require from leaders and staff? What would the impact be on staff, children, families, and the quality of the overall provision? Choose your own unique setting, specific behaviours or characteristics. I have given some examples below.

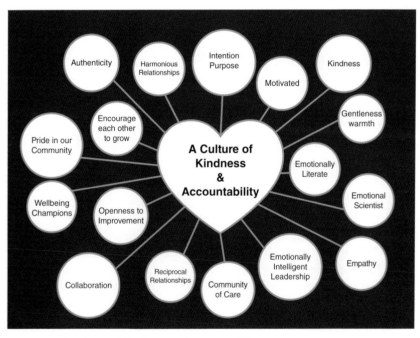

Figure 7.2 A culture of kindness and accountability

FINAL THOUGHTS

Workplace wellness toolkit
See pages 89–90 for a reminder of some ideas to create your own.

Have you identified any actions in the 'Core value: a culture of kindness and accountability' section that needs your attention?

References

Barside, S. & O'Neill, O. (2014). What's love got to do with it? A longitudinal study of the culture of companionate love and employee and client outcomes in a long-term care Setting. Available at: www.researchgate.net/publication/267869088_What's_Love_Got_to_Do_With_It_A_Longitudinal_Study_of_the_Culture_of_Companionate_Love_and_Employee_and_Client_Outcomes_in_a_Long-Term_Care_Setting

Brackett, M.A. (2019). *Permission to feel: unlocking the power of emotions to help our kids, ourselves, and our society thrive.* New York: Celadon Books.

Ofsted education inspection framework (EIF). (2019). Available at: https://www.gov.uk/government/publications/early-years-inspection-handbook-eif

Sincero, J. (2013). *You are a badass: how to stop doubting your greatness and start living an awesome life.* London: John Murray Learning.

A vision for the future: a mentally healthy early years workforce

Early years enthusiasts

I wanted to make sure that I have taken the opportunity I have been given to write this book, to do justice to a subject I am immensely passionate about. In order to do that, I knew it would not just involve my own experience or views of a sector that I am currently working in – in a hands-on, real-life practice kind of way. Knowing that our workforce is uniquely and beautifully diverse, I felt it especially important to seek the views of others and amplify others' lived experiences so we could see and hear from different perspectives of those that make up our workforce.

Whilst writing this book, I have enjoyed many enjoyable hours of telephone conversations and zoom calls with all of the talented and skilled early years professionals who so generously shared their experiences within the case studies of this book. I am incredibly grateful for their time and perspective. We have laughed and cried, shared sadness, connection, validity, joy, and tried to squeeze them all into these pages to give the subject of wellbeing true meaning and understanding, and hopefully do it justice. Perhaps this book may have also evoked emotions and feelings for you too. It is my hope that this leads to lasting change that positively impacts your own health and the health of the early years community in which you work and belong.

The true meaning of wellbeing

During the process of writing this book, I have discovered a new meaning of wellbeing. A meaning of wellbeing that truly means inclusion.

DOI: 10.4324/9781003146247-12

This is evident in the way this book has been formed and shaped by the many people who have contributed and provided their thoughts and feedback. This book was born from a desire to encourage others to put wellbeing at the heart of practice, perhaps to myth bust so as not to view wellbeing as something to tick off or complete, and only thought about haphazardly or by chance.

I hope it has shown more than that. When our starting point is the wellbeing of our community, starting with our educators, wellbeing becomes heart centric. It naturally guides us to a path that leads to connection and belonging. We can only ever feel that sense of belonging when we are authentically valued, respected, and included by shared core values and beliefs that form essential components of practice. That means no subjects are off-limits, and we have to get comfortable having uncomfortable conversations.

A community of care, belonging, and inclusion

I have long since wondered how we can care so passionately about children and then lack empathy for those we work with? Why do we ignore so much of who people are and at the same time hide away vast parts of ourselves? I hope this book has shown that when we embrace vulnerability and remove some of the armour we have used to protect ourselves, we can seek true purpose and connection. So often, what we feel are our most significant weaknesses are actually our greatest strengths. When we embrace all of the intersections of our identity and care to look and understand the intersections of the people we work with, that is where ordinary everyday magic can happen.

Our early years ecosystems of today are the workplaces for our children in the future. This brings us back to the enormous potential and legacy we can create collectively when we reach community actualisation and the pinnacle of a "breath of life". What type of legacy do we wish to leave?

How can I care so passionately about mental health awareness and fight for inclusion and speak out about stigma and discrimination and not care about other aspects of inequality in our world? The babies and children in our care grow up to be our adults of tomorrow. We let them go out into the world to face potential social injustice and inequity that may lead to bullying, trauma, victimisation, abuse, violence, poverty, poor housing, poorer educational outcomes that may affect their overall life chances.

Our mentally healthy early years workforce

Our vision for the future must involve the mental health of our early years workforce and must go beyond statutory and legal obligations. This can be achieved through training and all of us caring about each other and committing to the health and wellbeing of our workforce. That is why we all have to call for change. We have to create a collation of care. We can no longer afford to continue to leave health and wellbeing to chance.

We must be clear about increasing the mental health literacy of our workforce and creating zero stigma around mental health to safeguard the health of educators for the present and the future. We have learnt that mental ill-health is caused by a range of factors but that the environments in which we choose to work can significantly contribute to our overall health.

When we are skilled in spotting the warning signs of mental ill-health, we can provide early intervention and signpost for support as a method of prevention, so that we can reduce reactionary measures when we reach illness and crisis.

We also have to strive for a world where we understand being well and healthy is not about being symptom-free. Having a mental illness does not discount you from a career working with children or the opportunity to progress in your career. For too long, the stigma around mental health has led to a misunderstanding and prevented people from speaking out or receiving appropriate support within early years and education. When we work in environments with line managers who are comfortable speaking about mental health and can engage in uncomfortable conversations, they are better able to support their teams, which benefits all of our community, staff themselves, and the children and families in their care.

This kind of change will require and demand activism from us all, whether that is loudly making our voices known in view of many, or quietly in safer spaces away from public opinion. Nathan Archer (2021) prompts us to reflect on what early years activism looks like, how we can make our voices heard, and identify our values and principles for early education; not just for children and families but for ourselves. Understanding policy and what is driving policy change, defined as "critical literacy" (Sumsion, 2016 as cited by Archer, 2019), will allow us to make meaningful change and play a part politically. We may then begin to tackle the many factors that so often feel out of control, which so negatively impact our sector and directly influence our daily working role.

That is why this book must end with a call to action. A call to action to anyone that has read this book and wants to take deliberate steps that lead to greater job satisfaction, health, and happiness. I have set out a vision for the future and a mental wellbeing pledge that displays commitment and can lead to meaningful change.

A VISION for our future

V ocational training modules in EYE qualifications on mental health and wellbeing

I nclusive practice for EYE with mental health conditions

S tatutory mental health first aid training

I ncreased acceptance of mental health issues, including prevention and early intervention

O rganisational structures and systems that promote wellbeing protective factors

N etwork of early years mental health advocates – leading to a coalition of care

A mental wellbeing pledge

A pledge is a way to display your commitment to taking small steps leading to meaningful change. Let us think of it like a guide, the final stage in developing our workplace wellness toolkits, by incorporating our vision for the future of a mentally healthy early years workforce.

By signing this pledge, we commit to playing our part in making mental health a priority.

Our early years setting will:

1. Develop a personalised wellbeing manifesto that empowers staff to prioritise their mental wellbeing.
2. Take proactive steps to increase mental health awareness through everyday actions, personal and professional development opportunities.
3. Promote an open and honest culture around mental health that increases the mental health literacy of the community to eliminate stigma.
4. Consider the intersections of staff identities relating to wellbeing and culturally respectful practice.
5. Collate a workplace wellness toolkit with early intervention strategies, signposting to local and national organisations, and pathways for internal procedures, for example employee benefits, such as EAP.
6. Provide suitable working environments that promote work-life balance.
7. Ensure line managers and supervisors are trained and equipped to have supportive conversations on mental health.
8. Regularly seek feedback from staff on their health and wellbeing and evaluate the impact.
9. Create a network of wellbeing champions to empower our community to take care of themselves and look out for one another.
10. Keep up to date with, and where possible, actively inform the latest policy updates and share essential information for the wellbeing of the whole community.

Signed   Date

Final thoughts

This book started with a letter from me to you. Now I would like to ask you to write a letter to yourself. A note to your future self and all that you promise to do, be, and give yourself. Maybe it is to remind yourself of some of the valuable and meaningful reflections that have come to mind both personally and professionally that you may have considered throughout the chapters in this book. Write down all of your hopes and wellbeing wishes for your future health and happiness. The coalition of care has to start with ourselves so that we can bring all of ourselves to work and collectively cultivate community-actualisation.

References

Archer, Nathan (March, 2019). Hope and resilience in testing times. Available at: https://medium.com/children-s-centre/hope-and-resilience-in-testing-times-22d37b8c6af7

Archer, Nathan (February 22, 2021). Research: Action for change. Available at: www.earlyyearseducator.co.uk/features/article/research-action-for-change

Sumsion, J. (2006). From Whitlam to economic rationalism and beyond: A conceptual framework for political activism in children's services. *Australian Journal of Early Childhood*, 31(1), pp. 1–9.

LETTER TO MYSELF

_____

_____

_____

_____

_____

_____

_____

_____

_____

_____

_____

_____

_____

_____

_____

_____

_____

_____

_____

_____

_____

_____

_____

_____

Index

Page numbers in *italics* refer to figures, those in **bold** indicate tables.